OXFORD MORAL THEORY

Series Editor

David Copp, University of California, Davis

INNER VIRTUE

Nicolas Bommarito

OXFORD
UNIVERSITY PRESS

OXFORD
UNIVERSITY PRESS

Oxford University Press is a department of the University of Oxford. It furthers
the University's objective of excellence in research, scholarship, and education
by publishing worldwide. Oxford is a registered trade mark of Oxford University
Press in the UK and certain other countries.

Published in the United States of America by Oxford University Press
198 Madison Avenue, New York, NY 10016, United States of America.

Library of Congress Cataloging-in-Publication Data
Names: Bommarito, Nicolas, author.
Title: Inner virtue / by Nicolas Bommarito.
Description: New York : Oxford University Press, 2018. |
Series: Oxford moral theory
Identifiers: LCCN 2017011589 | ISBN 9780190673383 (hardcover : alk. paper)
Subjects: LCSH: Character. | Virtue.
Classification: LCC BJ1521 .B66 2017 | DDC 179/.9—dc23
LC record available at https://lccn.loc.gov/2017011589

1 3 5 7 9 8 6 4 2

Printed by Sheridan Books, Inc., United States of America

For all those with unseen goodness within

CONTENTS

ACKNOWLEDGMENTS

Nothing is possible without the proper conditions. With that in mind, I'd like to thank everyone who helped and encouraged me as I wrote this book.

Various institutions have supported me as I've thought through these ideas. As a graduate student I received support from Brown University and the Cogut Center for the Humanities. I also owe much to the philosophy department at New York University for awarding me a Bersoff Fellowship and to the University at Buffalo for granting me leave to accept it.

Many people have helped and encouraged me along the way. I'm especially grateful for the support of family and friends, particularly Charles Bommarito, Laura Bommarito, John Bommarito, and Michael Connolly.

I was sustained by many fellow philosophers while I struggled with writing: David Christensen, Jamie Dreier, Julia Driver, Jane Friedman, Jonardon Ganeri, Caspar Hare, Harvey Lederman, Béatrice Longuenesse, Jessica Moss, Regina Rini, Chelsea Rosenthal, Hagop Sarkissian, Josh Schechter, Sam Scheffler, Miriam Schoenfield, Whitney Schwab, Sharon Street, Jesse Summers, David Velleman, and Alex Worsnip.

I'm also grateful to my editor, Peter Ohlin, and to Tom Hurka and another referee for Oxford University Press, who all helped me to greatly improve the book.

Finally, thank you to those who helped and supported me most directly from the very earliest stages of work: Tim Schroeder (who saved me many times with his contagious optimism and creative problem solving), Dave Estlund (who is the very model of the analytic philosopher-gentleman), Jay Garfield (who took pity on me when I was a lost graduate student wandering India), Nomy Arpaly (who showed me what was possible in philosophy and continues to inspire, encourage, and challenge me every time we speak), and Alex King (who is the best partner in philosophy, academia, and life that I could ever ask for).

I'm so thankful to have you all in my life.

Men imagine that they communicate their virtue or vice only by overt actions, and do not see that virtue or vice emit a breath every moment.

—Ralph Waldo Emerson

Chapter 1

Introduction

Take a few seconds to think of the various people you have met in the course of your life. Of these people, pick one that you think deserves to be called a good person. This should not be some pious and preachy self-styled moralist, but a *genuinely good person*. One who inspires in you admiration and respect. The sort of person you bring to mind to combat the sneaking suspicion that humanity is nothing but selfish assholes, allowing you to say to yourself, "Well, not *everyone* is so bad."

Of course, we think of people like this as behaving in certain ways. They help us up when we fall, give to those in need, and say kind things to others. But we also expect them to have a certain kind of inner life: They won't experience disgust toward people of a certain race or contempt toward those who are weaker than they are. They will feel grateful for benefits they receive and sadness when confronted with various types of human misery. A good person won't merely *express* such states outwardly but will *experience* them inwardly—even when unable to express them.

Questions about the morality of action are, of course, interesting and important questions. In many cases a person's inner life doesn't matter much at all; I think people should not litter, but in this respect I care very little about the mental life of a stranger in the park, so long as their trash makes it into the garbage can. When I evaluate a *person*, however, it's a different story. It is not enough that my friend simply refrains from *making sexist comments*; it is important to me that he actually *lack a sexist outlook*. What I care about are my friend's inner mental features like his opinions, emotions, and desires.

One way to sharpen the point is to think of Robert Nozick's now infamous experience machine example. In the example, we must choose whether or not to be hooked up to a machine that hyperrealistically simulates any experience we'd like. One of the reasons to choose not to be hooked up to the machine, according to Nozick, is that doing so would destroy one's character. He writes,

> we want to *be* a certain way, to be a certain sort of person. Someone floating in a tank is an indeterminate blob. There is no answer to the question of what a person is like who has long been in the tank. Is he courageous, kind, intelligent, witty, loving? It's not merely that it's difficult to tell; there's no way he is.[1]

Leaving aside the question of whether or not one should choose to be hooked up to such a machine, it's worth considering what it would do to a person's moral character. According to Nozick, someone in the machine no longer has any character. For him, once in the machine, a jerk and a caring person are exactly the same—characterless blobs.

And yet those who enter the machine *can* still be better or worse in many ways. Some are nonmoral: An unimaginative person will

---

1. Nozick (1974, 43).

continue to be unimaginative, a clever person will still be clever, and a curious person will remain curious. Others are moral: Those who are jealous, spiteful, or cruel can be that way in the machine too. Those in the machine can still think and feel in ways that reflect poorly on their moral character.[2] One can feel the same feelings of racial contempt or schadenfreude in a simulated reality as in real life. Someone who takes great pleasure in experiencing a racially charged lynching in the machine is worse than someone whose pleasures don't involve such ill will. Seeing those in the machine as mere "blobs" ignores the many ways in which inner states are relevant to moral character.

OVERVIEW

In the broadest sense, the central question of the book is this: How does someone's inner life make them a morally better or worse person? Though my answer to this question will be crawling with the terms "virtue" and "vice," I must first admit that I have intense dislike for those terms and have turned to them as a last resort. For many of us, the very words are weighed down too heavily with baggage from ancient Greece to Christianity to Victorian England. When I talk of a vicious person, I do not mean to include someone who has a stutter or who smokes cigarettes; it has little to do with using swear words or wearing provocative clothing. When I talk of a virtuous person, I do not mean to conjure up images of virile "manly" men, chaste "pure" women, or holier-than-thou Puritans. One need not

---

2. This can also apply to "actions" performed within the machine. Committing a hyperrealistic, simulated rape reflects poorly on one's character. Julia Driver (2007) makes a similar point when she notes that immoral actions in a dream can reflect badly on one's character.

be Ned Flanders to count as a virtuous person. I use these terms primarily because if you want to write in English about what it means to be a morally good or bad person, those are the terms you're stuck with. It is my hope that a different picture of the "virtuous person" will emerge from my discussion—one that better resembles the people that inspire us and make life worthwhile.

I will not be engaged in many of the projects commonly associated with virtue talk. Virtue ethics is often dominated by lists, but I will not attempt to provide a complete list of virtues or even a list of cardinal virtues. My aim is to give an account of the role inner states play in making one a good person. My answer will not involve appealing to a list of morally good traits, but rather explaining what the items on such lists of morally good traits have in common.

Nor will I attempt to ground *all* of morality in the notions of virtue and vice; I will not attempt to derive other moral concepts like rights, well-being, blame, or obligation from virtue concepts.[3] I take virtue to be just *one part* of moral theory, though a rich and distinctive one. Questions about what makes a morally good person are important, but answering them does not provide the key to all other moral questions.

Because of recent work in the Aristotelian tradition, talk of virtues is strongly associated with a metaethical view that identifies goodness with natural human functioning.[4] Though I will call things good and bad, I will not rely on any particular account of the metaphysical nature of moral goodness or badness nor on any particular

---

3. Some theorists, such as Driver (1996, 111), draw a distinction between virtue *ethics* and virtue *theory*: The project of virtue ethics is to develop a theory of all of morality founded exclusively on virtues and vices, while the project of virtue theory is to provide an explanation of virtues and vices—the what, why, and when of being a good person. This work will be in the realm of virtue theory rather than virtue ethics.

4. See Philippa Foot (2001) and Rosalind Hursthouse (1999) for a defense of this kind of view.

semantics of the associated terms—this is a work in virtue theory, not in metaethical theory. Though I use a person's rights and well-being as paradigmatic cases of moral goods, my account of virtue does not depend on this. If you think there are clearer cases of moral goods, feel free to substitute in your favorite alternative.

Much discussion in virtue ethics, also inspired by Aristotle, is about what it means to live a flourishing human life. I will not assume that moral virtue is sufficient for the good life nor will notions of flourishing or the good life feature prominently in my discussion. I am concerned with the decidedly more narrow question of what it is to be a *morally* good person. Being a morally good person is compatible with being a better or worse person in many other respects.[5]

To talk of someone's character is to talk about what they are like, what sort of person they are. To talk of someone's *moral* character is to talk about what kind of person they are from the moral point of view. This is only a part of their overall character, one side of who they are, albeit a very important one. There are aspects of one's character, their sense of humor or their introversion, which are not part of their moral character. Having a sense of humor or being introverted does not make someone a morally better or worse person, even though those are important aspects of who they are. Again, my focus is on one's moral character, what kind of person someone is, *morally speaking.*

Virtue theory is, at its heart, about evaluating people. We talk about virtues and vices primarily as a way of making moral assessments of ourselves and others.[6] To say that generosity and kindness

---

5. Susan Wolf (1982) points out how moral virtue and living well more generally can be at odds by highlighting cases where those who are extremely moral often give up projects, pleasures, and relationships with nonmoral value.
6. This characterization is at odds with others, such as John Doris (2005) and Annette Baier (2008), who take virtues and vices to be primarily about predicting or explaining actions. We

are moral virtues is to say that these reflect well on a person's moral character. Virtues are traits that make a good person good; vices are traits that make a bad person bad. To say of a particular state or action that it is virtuous is to say that one is a (at least slightly) better person for it. An act of generosity is virtuous because doing so makes one a better person. Having a kind thought is virtuous because one is at least a slightly better person for having it.

This book has two main aims. The first is to establish a class of inner virtues and vices—states relevant to moral character that are independent of overt, voluntary action. It's not merely what we *do* that makes us virtuous or vicious but what happens to us on the inside; pleasure, emotion, and attention are all relevant to our moral character, even when confined to our inner lives. The second is to offer a substantive, unifying explanation of *how* these various inner states are virtuous or vicious; to explain what these diverse states all have in common that connects them to our moral character.

The essence of my answer is this: To be a good person is to care about moral goods. The most essential feature of a virtuous person is that moral goods like justice and the well-being of others matter to them—they care about such things.[7] Particular states (and actions too, though I will not focus on them) are virtuous by *manifesting* this care—by instantiating it in a particular way.

---

may use virtue talk in the task of making predictions, but that is at best a useful byproduct. If I want to *explain* why Jane returned the book, I'm willing to bet that action theorists have a better explanation than virtue ethicists.

7. My account is part of a more general family of accounts of virtue that link it with some positive orientation to moral goods. Thomas Hurka (2001) sees it as "loving the goods and hating evils," Robert Adams (2006) as "being for the good," and Nomy Arpaly and Timothy Schroeder (2014) as a special kind of intrinsic desire for the good. These accounts have also included discussions of inner states but have not focused on them. I don't mean to claim here that well-being and justice are the *only* moral goods; I just take them to be paradigmatic ones.

It is often natural to talk of particular virtues, to say that Mary is a generous person or that Michael is humble. I will take talk of virtues in general, things like gratitude or humility, to be derivative from particular virtuous states. These are complexes or patterns of states that have similar objects and similar domains—temperance involves a pattern of responses to consumables, patience involves responses to setbacks, and so on. In the case of inner virtues, these are patterns of inner states, mental and emotional responses to moral goods. To put it briefly: A virtuous person is someone who cares about moral goods, and a virtuous state is one that manifests such concern.

Things are a little more complicated in the case of vice. There are two ways to be a vicious person: One can lack concern for some moral goods, or one can care about things that are morally bad. Someone can be unjust by being indifferent to justice *or* by delighting in injustice.[8] Particular states are vicious by manifesting either indifference, a *lack* of concern for moral goods, or a positive, malicious concern for things that are morally bad.

Of course, many of these notions will require further unpacking—especially what it means to *care* about something and what it means for a state to *manifest* this care. Details aside, the essential point is what makes someone a morally good person is that morality *matters* to them in a deep way. Their actions and various aspects of their mental life are virtuous by embodying this concern. First, it will be important to clarify what inner virtues and vices are and why they are important.

8. Some, for example Julia Annas (2011, 102) and Gabriele Taylor (2006, 4–5), deny the existence of the latter type of vice. No one, they claim, *aims* to be vicious. It is not central to my account, but this strikes me as too naïve; many people have the positive aim of becoming less temperate (many college freshmen) or less honest (a budding con artist), often under that description. Aside from such examples, there are many sadistic and cruel people who are vicious even if they do not *aim* to be sadistic and cruel.

INNER VIRTUE AND ITS RELEVANCE

Inner virtues and vices are states relevant to moral character that do not require overt action. Overt action is what we normally think of when we think of actions; they are observable, voluntary bodily behaviors like eating lunch, reading a book, or playing a ukulele. These will contrast with covert actions—internal, mental actions like intentional attending, imagining, contemplating, or deliberating.

Covert actions are distinct from other involuntary mental phenomena, such as emotions or pleasures. Such states are not things we *do*, but things that happen to us. Many of the states I will focus on are not doings at all; feeling jealousy, pleasure, or anger is not something we *do*, though we may do things to encourage or avoid such feelings.

Many states blur the line between voluntary and involuntary. Consider things like breathing or blinking. Most of the time these are automatic events, though if we choose, we can intentionally decide to take deep breaths or blink rapidly. Similarly, sometimes thinking, remembering, or attending is an action, something that I *do*. Other times, however, it is something that *happens to me*. I can try to remember who sat next to me in algebra class or decide to think about my bank account balance. However, the memory of a classmate can also pop into my head, and thoughts about my financial situation can force themselves upon me. Though my discussion will focus on involuntary inner states, much of what I claim will also apply to covert, inner action.

Voluntary or not, what these inner states have in common is that they need not be displayed externally in our overt behavior. Even though they may be commonly associated with overt actions, they are distinct from externally observable changes in conduct. One can be pleased to hear of a colleague's misfortune without expressing it. One can feel annoyed with a loudmouthed friend without showing it. One can miss a recently deceased friend terribly while keeping all outside appearances as usual. There's a world of difference between *being angry* and *behaving angrily*, between *feeling grateful* and *expressing gratitude*. Though they may normally go together, it's easy to have one without the other.

After discussing inner virtue and vice more generally, I will discuss a variety of mental states in detail. I will defend a variety of particular claims about how, when, and why pleasure, emotion, and conscious attention are relevant to our moral character. What these different types of inner states have in common, I will argue, is that they are all ways that our moral cares or concerns manifest in our mental lives. This explanation illuminates how such a wide variety of inner states can all be virtuous or vicious, how they can all be connected to our moral character.

Inner virtues and vices have both practical and theoretical significance. They are, of course, themselves an important area of moral life, one that has been neglected in recent English-language moral thought. Theorizing about inner virtue highlights the fact that there is more to a person's moral character than their actions and the mental states that accompany them.

Despite how it may seem, inner virtues and vices *are* relevant to everyday practice. Moral development, for example, looks quite different when you aim at cultivating not only certain intentions and overt actions but also at developing pleasures, emotions, thoughts, and habits of attention, many of which may not be outwardly displayed. Keeping in mind the importance of such inner states can also drastically alter our confidence when making moral assessments of others. Seeing the ways in which we all have morally relevant states that are not easily seen from the outside should make us much more cautious when making such judgments about others.

Ignoring inner states in moral theory can make it tempting to think that a theory of virtue is parasitic on a theory of right or praise-worthy action. Without inner virtues, it can seem as though if we had a complete theory of morally good action, we would get a complete theory of virtue for free—the virtuous person would simply be someone who reliably performs those actions (or at least *intends* to perform them). The existence of inner virtues and vices shows that an account of what it is to be a virtuous person is not a corollary of an account of right action. It is a distinct mode of moral evaluation of its own.

Chapter 2

Inner Virtue and Vice

Recently, ethical theory has been an action-packed discipline. Not because ethics conferences feature car chases or gunfights, but because most discussion focuses on questions about what to *do*. "Which actions," most theorists wonder, "are permissible and which are obligatory? Which are blameworthy?" For many, these are *the* questions that constitute ethics as a discipline; it is seen as a field where we think about moral *agents* and what they should or should not *do*. Allan Gibbard puts this point of view plainly when he writes, "Ethics concerns what to do."[1]

This view of ethics is so pervasive that many philosophers will use the terms "agent" and "person" interchangeably. When inner states are discussed, they tend to be those connected directly with deliberate overt action, such as motives and intentions. I wish to suggest that this focus is a mistake—our inner lives are an interesting and ineliminable part of moral theory, even when involuntary or disconnected from outward behaviors.[2]

---

1. Gibbard (2003, 13). Here he is echoing G. E. Moore from the first chapter of his *Principia Ethica*: "For when we say that a man is good, we commonly mean that he acts rightly; when we say that drunkenness is a vice, we commonly mean that to get drunk is a wrong or wicked action. And this discussion of human conduct is, in fact, that with which the name Ethics is most intimately associated."

2. Somewhat surprisingly, the virtue ethics literature has also been guilty of excessive focus on voluntary action. Rosalind Hursthouse's (1996, 1999) attempt to show that virtue ethics *can*

Along with this view of ethics as a subject comes a particular way of understanding what it means to be a virtuous person. If ethics is about what to do, then being a morally good person is simply a matter of doing or not doing certain actions. On this approach to moral theory, once we have an account of right action, we get an account of the virtuous person for free: The virtuous person is just someone who does (or is at least *disposed* to do) the morally right actions.

We can include more than a few illustrious thinkers among those who think of virtue in this way: G. E. Moore writes that virtue "may be defined as an habitual disposition to *perform certain actions*" (1903/1993, 221). Henry Sidgwick (1907/1982, 219) defines virtues as "qualities exhibited in *right conduct*" and W. D. Ross (1936/1963, 292) identifies virtue with "tendencies to *behave*." Other prominent proponents of this view include John Rawls, who claims virtues are "sentiments and habitual attitudes leading us to act on certain principles of right" (1971/1999, 383) and Bernard Williams, who calls virtue "a disposition of character to choose or reject *actions* because they are of a certain ethically relevant kind" (1985/1998, 8–9).

This view also appears in more recent philosophical work. So we find Owen Flanagan claiming, "On every view the virtues are psychological dispositions *productive of behavior*" (1991, 282). Gilbert Harman has a similar view, describing virtues as "relatively long-term stable disposition to act in distinctive ways. An honest person is disposed to act honestly. A kind person is disposed to act kindly" (1999, 317). As Harman's comments suggest, this also comes up in discussions of particular virtues: So, for example, Elizabeth Anscombe

give us advice on how to act, that it provides action-guiding "v-rules," has generated much discussion. For just a recent slice, see Everitt (2007), Russell (2009), van Zyl (2009 and 2011), Hurka (2010), Stangl (2010), and Svensson (2010). See also Hacker-Wright (2010), who contrasts the role of right action in Foot and Anscombe with more recent work in virtue ethics.

(1958/1997, 43) and Judith Jarvis Thompson (1997, 280) both take a just person to simply be someone prone to performing just acts; George Sher (2002, 385) makes similar claims about a kind person.[3]

This is not to suggest that this view of the virtuous person is limited to English-language philosophers in the last hundred years. We can also find it in the *Brihadaranyaka Upanishad*, an early Indian philosophical text, where many passages explicitly claim that a person is made good by good actions and bad by bad actions.[4] Without belaboring the point, conceiving of the virtuous person in this way, as simply someone who behaves in certain ways, has been very popular for a variety of theorists.

And yet, there *is* much more to moral character than our overt actions. To see this, it will be useful to borrow an example from the philosophy of mind literature; consider a variation of fictional creatures imagined by Galen Strawson:

Weather Watchers: Though appearing to us as giant stone monoliths, they are living creatures with mental lives much

---

3. The emphasis in all of these quotations is mine. It should be noted that some theorists seem to have this view in some places, but not others. Though Aristotle tells us that it is how we behave in our dealings with others that makes some people just and others unjust and what we do in terrifying situations that makes some people brave and others cowardly (*NE* 1103b14–17), he continues to say that this also applies to our appetites and to emotions such as anger (*NE* 1103b17–18). These states, however, are usually talked about in conjunction with overt action, as when he emphasizes that the continent person is different from the virtuous person (*NE* 1102b26–8 and 1151b43ff); performing a virtuous action is not the same as merely acting in accordance with virtue (*NE* 1105a33). This also happens in non-Aristotelian theory; Julia Driver describes virtue as a disposition to "produce intentional action" (2001, 25 and 107) and claims, "what is crucial is whether or not the person is *disposed* to act well" (2001, 53). However, she also talks about them as dispositions to "feel, behave, or act well" (1996, 124) and describes blind charity as a virtue "in thought rather than in deed" (2001, 28). More recently, she writes, "even when utterly ineffective, we admire good attitudes" (2016, 110). Robert Adams (2006) and Julia Annas (2011) also make claims about virtue that seem to vary in this respect.

4. See *Brihadaranyaka Upanishad* 3.2.13 and 4.4.5, among other passages.

like our own—they have thoughts, memories, desires, emotions, sensations, and even fantasies and dreams. These
creatures care very deeply about the weather; they are filled
with joy when it is sunny out and melancholy when it rains
or snows. Because of their physiology, they are completely
incapable of any behavioral action—their rigid, heavy bodies are too firmly rooted to the ground to allow for any movement. Nevertheless, they do have various ways to sense the
weather: Their hard exteriors can detect moisture, tempera-
ture, and even subtle pressure changes. Their stationary com-
pound eyes are very perceptive and can see quite well in many
directions at once. However, none of their rich mental lives
are externally observable and, because of the kind of creatures
they are, they are unable to perform overt actions of any kind.
From the outside they are immobile sculptures, but internally
they are very much alive.[5]

Just as beings like us cannot fly through the air unaided, see ultraviolet light, or be physically present in two places at the same time,
Weather Watchers cannot do things like run away from the rain
or physically harm another Weather Watcher. They will even lack
the associated intentions—human beings may *wish* for or *dream* of
being in two places at once or seeing ultraviolet light, but cannot
plan or *intend* to do such things. So, too, with Weather Watchers;
they may wish they could run from the rain or dream of rolling
around in the sunshine, but they cannot do such things nor have the
associated intentions.

In an extreme version of the case, Weather Watchers cannot
even perform covert actions like performing mental arithmetic

---

5. This is my own description inspired by the one found in Strawson (1994, 251ff.).

or voluntarily focusing their attention; they cannot have intentions and are not rightly called agents at all. Such extreme Weather Watchers could be morally assessable by having the kinds of inner, involuntary states I will emphasize. Because my focus is on inner states more generally, I will stick to the less extreme case of Weather Watchers who can perform inner, covert actions (and have the associated intentions) but cannot perform or intend overt, external actions. It is worth keeping in mind that many of the states I will focus on are morally assessable independently of any associated covert actions.

If moral character is determined by our overt actions, then Weather Watchers will turn out to be completely amoral beings. If being virtuous is just a matter of reliably doing morally good actions, then Weather Watchers are neither virtuous nor vicious. Evaluated in this way, they seem to be, as Nozick might say, mere blobs. After all, they cannot help or harm anyone. They cannot make, steal, or donate anything; they cannot murder, rescue, cheat, help, or abuse anyone. Whatever psychological tendencies they have, they are not productive of behavior. If morality is about telling us what we should *do*, then morality seems to have little to say about creatures like Weather Watchers.

And yet, though unable to perform overt actions, there are many ways in which Weather Watchers *can* be morally virtuous or vicious. Just as they can feel relief when a storm is over and anxiety when there are dark clouds on the horizon, Weather Watchers can feel sorrow and grief over the fact that some of their fellow creatures are rooted in horrible climates, enduring near constant rainfall. A Weather Watcher can feel envious of another's sunny location or take malevolent pleasure in seeing a fellow Weather Watcher getting soaked in a storm. Or if, after such an intense storm, a fallen tree obscures the view of other Weather Watchers, one may wonder how the others are doing and worry about their well-being. They are capable of feeling disgust and contempt for Weather Watchers that are missing an eye or deformed in some other way. Just as they might vividly imagine a sunny day in the midst of a terrible storm, they are capable of dwelling in gruesome and graphic fantasies involving the torment of their neighbors.

These features of inner life make a Weather Watcher morally better or worse despite not involving overt action and, in many cases, not involving action at all. Even without the ability to perform overt actions, Weather Watchers can have moral character. Their inner lives afford them a wide variety of ways of being virtuous or vicious. If there were a heaven and hell for Weather Watchers, the deity in charge of passing judgment would not be forced to abstain, with a divine shrug of the shoulders, because there is nothing for her to judge. Rather, there are a wide variety of features of their inner lives that would allow her to sort the good-hearted ones from the wicked.

Talk of imaginary creatures like Weather Watchers is likely to strike many as simply too outlandish. It can feel like a stretch to suppose that science-fiction scenarios involving bizarre, sentient statues can tell us anything about moral character in flesh-and-blood human beings.[6] There is something to this sentiment; after all, what we think of as virtuous and vicious often depends on the kind of creatures we are. If we were not the kind of beings who consume food and drink, there would be no such virtue as temperance. If we were not the kinds of beings that experience fear, we would not

---

6. Philippa Foot (1979, 8–14), for example, claims that virtues counter common *human* temptations to vice. She uses the example of courage; if humans had no temptation to run from danger or avoid painful facts, there would be no such virtue as courage. This notion of courage strikes me as far too narrow—after all, a Weather Watcher could courageously face an impending hurricane despite being unable to run away. I am, however, sympathetic with the general spirit of her claim.

include courage among our virtues. Radically different kinds of beings, Weather Watchers included, are apt to have radically different virtues and vices. Nevertheless, it is striking that we *can* share many virtues and vices with these radically different beings, despite their lack of overt action.

There are, however, more realistic cases of this kind involving actual human beings. Consider the real-life condition known as locked-in syndrome.[7] This tragic condition is a type of full-body paralysis often caused by a stroke or brain injury. Though it renders the body almost entirely immobile, it does not interfere with cognitive functioning or consciousness. The following is a fictionalized case based on the medical literature and memoirs written by those with locked-in syndrome:

> **Locked-In:** Before the stroke, the majority of Roger's life had been fairly typical for a middle-aged North American. Though not without his faults, Roger was always quick with a sincere, kind word; in fact, he seemed to have a preternatural sense for when such words were needed most. He was also a patient and empathetic listener, a trait that many of his acquaintances admit helped them through very tough times. This isn't to say he was always a perfect saint, but most who know him would say he was a pretty good person. One day while working in his garden, Roger suffered a stroke. After being rushed to the hospital, he was comatose for a few days. Once he awoke, he found himself trapped in his own body, unable to move or communicate at all. Despite the lack of evidence to the contrary, Roger's

---

7. This condition is referred to by various technical names: cerebromedullospinal disconnection, de-efferented state, pseudocoma, ventral pontine syndrome, and pontine disconnection syndrome (among others). For an overview of the medical literature on this condition, see Patterson and Grabois (1986) and Laureys et al. (2005).

family felt strongly that he was not in a vegetative state; they could somehow sense that he was still with them. Various scans of Roger's brain confirmed what his family had suspected, that Roger's higher brain functions were completely intact. He was fully conscious and able to see, hear, and understand the world just as well as he did before the stroke. Outwardly he appeared as if he was in a coma, but inwardly he was the same as he always had been.

In the most common version of the syndrome, what is known as "classical" locked-in syndrome, the person is able to blink and move their eyes vertically. It is from this type of case that most firsthand accounts of the condition are drawn, often written via a painstaking system of blinks.[8] There is, however, another more severe version of the syndrome, known as "total" or "complete" locked-in syndrome, where the person has no motor control at all and is completely unable to move or communicate.[9] As you might imagine, this is very difficult to diagnose and is often only detectable through scanning the brain in various ways.[10]

So, like the Weather Watchers, Roger cannot perform overt actions of any kind. The prognosis for those with locked-in syndrome is, at least for now, quite poor. We can suppose that Roger knows that, in his particular case, there is no hope of recovering any of his motor skills. Roger, like the Weather Watchers, has a rich inner life while being unable to perform any overt actions.

8. Perhaps the most famous firsthand account is Jean-Dominique Bauby's *The Diving-Bell and the Butterfly* (1997/2007). See Tavalaro and Tayson (1997), Chisholm and Gillett (2005), and Pistorius (2013) for others.
9. This classification originates from Bauer et al. (1979). See also Patterson and Grabois (1986, 758).
10. For more detail on the methods of diagnosing locked-in syndrome, see Kotchoubey and Lotze (2013).

Things may be a bit more complicated for Roger when it comes to intentions. Though, like Weather Watchers, Roger knows that he cannot perform overt actions, unlike Weather Watchers he has not *always* been that way. Rather than *instantly* losing the ability to form intentions or plans to perform overt actions, it is more likely that there is a difficult transition period. One locked-in patient, Martin Pistorius, describes this period of adjustment to the loss of control of his body (his case involved not only paralysis but involuntary spasms as well):

> Even as I became aware, I didn't fully understand what had happened to me. Just as a baby isn't born knowing it can't control its movement or speak, I didn't think about what I could or couldn't do. Thoughts rushed through my mind that I never considered speaking, and I didn't realize the body I saw jerking or motionless around me was mine. It took time to understand I was completely alone in the middle of a sea of people. But as my awareness and memories slowly started to mesh together, and my mind gradually reconnected to my body, I began to understand I was different. Lying on the sofa as my father watched gymnastics on TV, I was fascinated by the bodies that moved so effortlessly, the strength and power they revealed in every twist and turn. Then I looked down at a pair of feet I often saw and realized they belonged to me. It was the same with the two hands that trembled constantly whenever I saw them nearby. They were part of me too, but I couldn't control them.[11]

Even if Roger is initially still able to form intentions for overt behavior, after some time he will no longer do so and his mental life will resemble the fictional Weather Watchers much more closely.

11. Pistorius (2013, 13).

This does seem to mean that there are virtues that Roger can no longer have. If generosity requires overt gift giving, then he can no longer be generous. If honesty requires the ability to communicate with others, then he can no longer be honest. If benevolence requires acting to help others, he can no longer be benevolent. Virtues that require overt behavior, or at least the intention to perform such behaviors, are not open to those with locked-in syndrome.

And yet it is not as if the *entirety* of Roger's moral character was annihilated the moment he had the stroke. If Roger was racist before the stroke, he is still racist after it, too. If he was thoughtful or patient before, he is now a thoughtful or patient person who happens to have locked-in syndrome. He can still feel admiration, schadenfreude, envy, and gratitude. He can still face his future with courage, resentment, or bitterness. These inner states can all reflect on his moral character, even though they can no longer manifest externally.

This is not to say that inner life is the *only* thing that matters for moral character. For nearly all of us, an important challenge to being a good person is integrating our inner lives with our overt, public behaviors. Weather Watchers and those with locked-in syndrome are, to be sure, extreme cases, but there are often important general insights to be gained by considering extreme cases. Their moral life is truncated in important ways, but it is not extinguished. And yet the aspects of moral life that remain are present in us, too. Thinking about these extreme cases can help us to see the aspects of our moral character that are independent of overt action.

VIRTUE, DISPOSITIONS, AND RELIABILITY

Roger can be morally virtuous in various ways, despite being unable to perform any overt actions. This shows that there are virtues that do not require overt behavior. Those wishing to resist this might respond by appeal to dispositions: Roger can't perform overt actions anymore, but he can still be *disposed* to do these things. The reason that virtues are still open to him is that he is still disposed to do many behavioral actions, but because of his illness, he is unable to actually do them.

What does it mean to say that Roger has a disposition to perform certain overt actions? He is not disposed to act in the everyday sense of the word; it's odd to say that he is *apt* to jump up and down or that he has a *tendency* to walk across the room. But it would be too quick to say that we cannot be disposed to do things that we are unable to do: I can be disposed to visit a coffee shop even if my car is broken and there is no coffee shop within walking distance. But this seems to rely on a *general* ability to visit coffee shops. I cannot be disposed to visit Neptune not simply because I can't visit Neptune *today* or *this week*, but because I can *never* do so.

The mere fact that Roger *would* do many actions *if he could* is not sufficient to attribute dispositions for overt action to him. This would be far too strong. Though I *would* fly to class each day if I had wings, I am not disposed to fly to class. Though I *would* rattle off the first thousand prime numbers if I could, I am not disposed to do so. If being disposed to do something simply means that I would do it if I were just a little different, then it seems everyone is disposed act morally; after all, if their cares, desires, and beliefs were different, then they would perform good actions for the right reasons. Even worse, everyone is, for similar reasons, also disposed to act *immorally* at the same time.

One way to understand Roger is to see him as someone who has had the part of his brain that connects beliefs and desires to bodily action completely removed. In the same way that an apple with its core removed is no longer disposed to sprout into an apple tree, a person with the bodily-action core removed is no longer disposed to perform such actions. And for those like Roger, the removal of this core does not amount to the removal of the entirety of his moral character.[12]

It's worth noting that *even if* we grant that Roger does have behavioral dispositions, there are still a variety of virtues and vices open to him that can be explained without any reference to such dispositions. So rather than debating whether or not Roger can have dispositions to behave, it is worth asking why it is tempting to talk of dispositions when discussing virtues and vices in the first place. It is not because dispositions are particularly elegant or illuminating explanatory tools. Explaining John's generosity via his disposition to give gifts sounds a lot like explaining the medicine's sedative properties via its disposition to cause sleep.[13] At least at the macro-level of psychology and moral theory, dispositions are less like explanations and more like placeholders for an explanation. Since I'm in the business of explaining virtuous states, I will avoid talk of dispositions (what *would* happen in certain circumstances) and instead focus on the occurrent features of a person that *explain* these dispositions. In particular, I'll focus on how a particular underlying occurrent state, care or concern, can explain how states are virtuous or vicious.

Of course, philosophers writing about virtue don't invoke dispositions for no reason; the very purpose of attributing virtues and vices lends itself to talk of dispositions. Virtue is about evaluating persons, and so involves a general assessment of someone over time. If I wonder whether or not Emily is a good person, I'm not wondering about how she is *today* or *at this moment* (though those are relevant!), but what kind of person she is *in general*. Sometimes events

12. I thank Tim Schroeder for this analogy.
13. This originates from Moliére's play *Le Malade Imaginaire*, where a physician explains that opium makes one sleepy because it has the *virtus dormitiva*, or "dormitive virtue."

from the past are relevant ("Even as a child she was so thoughtful") and sometimes they are not ("That was just how she was as an angsty teenager"). To make this kind of general evaluation, it is helpful to appeal to some *persisting, stable* feature of the person. Dispositions offer such stability—saying a dog is loud or excitable means that it tends to make noise in many situations. This is a stable and persisting feature of the dog because we can say it is loud or excitable even if it is currently napping quietly.[14]

This can make it tempting to see the stability associated with virtue to be straightforwardly statistical: In the same way that a loud dog is one that often barks, for someone to have a virtue is just for them to often exhibit the trait in the appropriate situation. On this view, we could know who has reliable or stable honest tendencies simply by getting statistics on how often they behaved honestly. But as many sports fans know, such overall stats can be misleading. Consider the notion of a "clutch player"—such a player performs well *when the stakes are high.* Other players may have better overall stats than the clutch player—that is, their tendency to score is more stable and reliable—but the small percentage of situations where they fail includes the important ones when the game is on the line.[15]

We can imagine a moral version of our clutch player who, though her overall honesty or bravery "stats" are lower, she is able to

---

14. When defending virtue as a disposition, Julia Annas (2011, 8–10) talks about how we want virtue to be "persisting" and "reliable"; recall that Aristotle thought virtue was a *hexis*—a settled state. Robert Adams often talks about virtue being a "persisting" state and muses about the vagueness of this persistence, claiming that a day would not be enough, but five years might do the trick (2006, 18).

15. The classic example in baseball of a clutch player is Reggie Jackson, who earned the nickname "Mr. October" for his improved postseason performance. Statistical evidence for the existence of clutch players is controversial, in part because determining what exactly counts as a clutch situation is fairly complicated. Hibbs (2010) argues that statistical analysis is sufficient to determine who is a clutch player, and Winston (2012) uses statistical methods to argue that Tony Pérez was one such clutch player. Thanks to Don Garrett and Jamie Dreier for help with these issues.

be honesty and courageous "when the chips are down." Her moral stats are worse in that she acts bravely or honestly less frequently and less reliably than others. However, the times when she *does* act bravely or honestly are in situations when it really counts and when others find it difficult. It is difficult to tell whether a clutch baseball player is a better overall player than a more statistically reliable teammate, but it can seem so in the moral case: Would you rather your child grow up to be someone with clutch honesty or someone with better honesty stats but who fails to be honest in important situations?

The reason that in the moral case the clutch player seems better is because her honesty or courage in difficult or high-stakes situations reflects a deeper commitment to morality. Not all reliability is the same; what we want in a virtuous person is a *depth of concern*. Caring deeply about something is often associated with stability or reliability, but stability is insufficient for it. Of two professors who have never missed a class, both have reliable and stable tendencies. However, one might be a deeply committed educator, while the other is simply stuck in a rut. Or, as Nomy Arpaly puts it: In a calm climate, fair-weather friends can stick around for years.[16] Good friends stick around, but not everyone who sticks around is a good friend.

The same is true for inner states—simply reliably having compassionate feelings is not enough to make someone virtuous. Suppose a well-intentioned scientist kidnaps me and implants a device that randomly but frequently stimulates my brain in a way that gives me compassionate feelings. The device is quite reliable and gives me a stable psychological disposition to feel compassionate feelings toward others. If being reliably disposed to have compassionate feelings is all that matters, the scientist has thereby made me a fully

16. Arpaly (2004, 94).

compassionate person. There is, however, an important difference between me and someone who has reliable compassionate feelings *because the sufferings of others matter to them.* Though we both have reliable and stable psychological tendencies, mine is shallow in a way that theirs is not—theirs is grounded in a particular orientation to the good, one that responds to the well-being of others. I have compassionate feelings because of the implant, whereas they have such feelings because they genuinely care about other people. Even if they have compassionate feelings less reliably than I do, they are still more virtuous than I am. Stability is important, but it is not all that we want when it comes to virtue.[17]

What is important is how the particular compassionate feelings are connected with our deepest cares and concerns. When my feelings are caused by an implant, they aren't happening because I care about other people and so they don't reflect anything about my moral character. In most cases, a virtuous person will have a variety of behavioral, emotional, and attentional dispositions. Many of them are nonmoral and irrelevant to moral evaluations of the person. Someone might be disposed to tie their shoes in a certain way or to feel a bit down on rainy days; such dispositions don't say anything about their moral character.

When morally relevant, what explains these tendencies and their stability is an underlying stable and persisting state—moral care or concern. The reason that a virtuous person has a long-term tendency to be generous or to feel compassion for others is their deep concern for the well-being of others. Just as a devoted friend's

17. Of course, if the device actually triggers genuine, but momentary concern, the compassionate feelings would be fully virtuous. Insofar as this device makes the suffering of others actually matter to me, the device does seem to make me morally virtuous. When evaluating my character over time, however, I may still fall short of being fully virtuous because the concern is fleeting and unstable. As I will discuss, this is not necessarily because stability itself is good (though it might be!), but may be a result of the psychological fact that our deepest concerns tend to be stable.

concern explains why she tends to be there for someone, a virtuous person's moral concern explains why they tend to be generous and feel compassionate feelings. As Weather Watchers and cases of locked-in syndrome show, this underlying state *can* be manifested in overt behavior, but it need not be.

CARE AND CONCERN

We all know what it is to care about something. A key concept in my account of how inner states can be virtuous or vicious is the notion of care or concern (I will use the terms interchangeably).[18] I use these terms in a largely nontechnical sense, as when we say "Joan cares about her children" or "I'm concerned about finding a job." Having care or concern for these things means they *matter* to us, that they are important to us. Though we've all experienced what it is to care about something, it will be worth highlighting some of its key features.

Caring about something does not entail that you *realize* that you care about it. We can be mistaken about what matters to us. Someone who has moved away from a city might find that he doesn't care about fine dining as much as he thought. Someone's friends may see that her art really matters to her, even though she sees it as a relatively unimportant hobby. Caring is about what matters to you, not what you *believe* about what matters to you.

Care and concern are aimed at a wide variety of objects; this differentiates it from other, more restricted, neighboring concepts in ethical theory. Many moral theories that focus on care take it to be a social

---

18. My discussion of care and concern here, particularly how they might be distinct from desire, preference, and judgment draws much from Harry Frankfurt (1982/1988 and 1999) and Stephen Darwall (1997/1998 and 2002). See also Maguire (2016), who makes use of a similar notion of care.

relationship between persons; on these views, the object of care must be another *person*.[19] Care, as I will use it, includes this type of interpersonal care, but is much broader in scope. On my use, we can care not only about people but also about ideas, objects, and states of affairs.

For the same reason, care is also distinct from desire. Caring about something involves having certain desires, but it is not the same as desire. Desires are, for example, commonly taken to be directed only toward states of affairs; when I desire some chocolate, my desire is for the world to be a certain way, for it to be the kind of world where I am eating some chocolate.[20] Even though caring about my mother will involve a constellation of desires, for her health and happiness, saying that I care about her is not the same as saying that I desire the states of affairs that promote her health or happiness. My care is aimed more directly at *her*, the person sitting in front of me. Though we often care about how the world is, we also care about people in a more direct way.

There are, then, many different objects of our care and concern. We can, after all, care about many different types of things. We care about particular people and states of affairs but also about ideas, rules, events, symbols, and physical objects. Someone can care, for example, about their brother, the ideal of equality, a note written by a deceased friend, the political situation in Nepal, getting a promotion, and so on—a variety of different types of things. When someone cares about mathematics, ballet, or philosophy, they do not simply care about the people engaged in the activity, but also about a general practice. To care about freedom or equality is not simply to care about disadvantaged or imprisoned people but also about an abstract ideal.

19. This notion of care can be found in Noddings (1984/2003), Held (2006), Darwall (2002), and Slote (2007).
20. This notion of desire, though common, has been disputed; see Thagard (2006).

Often these different objects of concern are mixed together. Many concerns that initially seem singular can involve diverse types of objects. If a devout Muslim cares about the *Qur'an*, what does he care about? It is likely to be many things—he can care about an abstract text, the meaning of this text, a vocalized performance of the text, the cultural practice of these recitations, the particular physical edition that his father gave him, or the states of affairs in which more people read and reflect on the text. Likely, his care will involve a mix of all of these different objects.

This kind of care or concern is a long-term, persisting feature of a person. It is unlike the particular local mental states that it gives rise to like pleasures, emotions, or thoughts. This isn't to deny that cares do arise and pass away—a passionate lawyer may care deeply about legal theory, even though she did not *always* care about it. An ex-swimmer may no longer care about competitive swimming, though he cared deeply about it in his teenage years. It is similar to other more general features: A person has a particular gender, is outgoing, confident, intelligent, and so on. We rightly ascribe these features to people even when they are not currently manifesting them, say, when in dreamless sleep. In the same way, Ben cares about his mother and about social justice even when he is currently asleep, in bed with a cold, or watching a movie. His concern is a persisting, underlying state; a fundamental orientation he has to the world.

Some philosophers take persistence through time to be part of what it means to care about something. There is something to this. When we try to imagine instantaneous, fleeting care, it seems less like caring and more like an impulse.[21] It may, however, be possible to imagine a person who cares about different things with each new

21. This point is made by Frankfurt (1982/1988, 84). Robert Solomon makes a similar point: To say "He loves passionately, but only for a few minutes at a time" is most likely to make a biting joke (1998, 94).

hour or day. When considering this strange person, it can be hard to accept that their momentary cares are very deep. This is likely because of the contingent psychological fact that our cares and concerns, especially the deep ones, tend not to just pop in and out of existence. Deep concerns, for most of us, tend to stick around. As anyone who has changed careers or ended a relationship can tell you, shaking a deep concern can be a very difficult task. If only for psychological reasons, cares and concerns are persisting states, a general orientation we have toward the world.

It is also important to distinguish caring from reflective judgments of value. One can judge avant-garde interpretive dance, scholarship on economics in the history of Latvia, or advanced medical techniques to treat cystic fibrosis to be *valuable* without *caring* about them. "I'm really glad these things exist," we might say, "but they don't really matter much to me."

Judgment is also different from care in that it is a conscious, reflective process. This need not be true of caring—I may care about an acquaintance or getting a promotion without consciously realizing that I care about these things. Though I'll argue that what we care about often affects our conscious experience, particularly our patterns of attention, caring about something is not the same as reflective judgment of its value. We often care about things or relationships that we would (rightly or wrongly!) reflectively judge to be without much value.

Preferences, desires, and judgments of value are, of course, closely associated with care or concern. Caring about something typically involves judgments of value and having certain desires and preferences regarding it. As I'll discuss in detail, it also has a close relationship with our pleasures, emotions, and conscious attention. These various mental states are not, however, identical with care. As I'll use the term, caring about something is an underlying, typically long-term, positive orientation to something. This involves some personal investment or identification with the object. To care about something means that it *matters* or is *important* to you in a deep way.

MORAL VIRTUE AS THE MANIFESTATION OF CARE

Roger and the Weather Watchers can be morally virtuous because they are able to care about moral goods—things like the rights and well-being of others can still matter to them. Though such concerns cannot manifest as behavior, they can manifest in their mental lives—as pleasure, displeasure, emotion, and conscious attention. They may not be full *agents* in the same way that most of us are, but they are moral beings nevertheless.

It is this concern that is the very heart of being a morally good person; particular states are virtuous derivatively, via their connection with this concern. This account of moral virtue provides the best explanation of how and why various inner states count as morally virtuous or vicious. This will become clear in my treatment of particular inner states, but first it will be useful to clarify the relation between moral concern and particular states.[22]

It is natural to think that our concern both causes and explains particular states. This is common in everyday explanations: We say things like, "She feels anxious about the interview because she cares about getting the job" or "He's pleased about the sale because

---

22. Though care or concern is a persisting orientation toward the world, we can still evaluate particular instances of care or concern. Is Ben's concern for justice genuine? Does he *really* care *right now, at this very moment*? These are legitimate evaluations, but we most often ask these questions in the service of evaluating persons. We wonder if Ben really cares because we want to figure out what we think of *Ben*. This is why I focus on evaluating persons and not particular instances of care or concern.

he cares about saving money." In these cases, the underlying care both produces the state and helps us to understand why the person experiences it.

The particular feeling of anxiety or pleasure also *says* something about the person because it is connected with their underlying cares and concerns. Part of the role of calling states virtuous is to link them to one's moral character—they say something about what kind of person someone is. When the underlying care or concern is *moral* in nature, when it is about moral values like equality, justice, or the well-being of others, the particular states say something about one's moral character. So when Ben feels indignation about unsafe working conditions because he cares about the rights and well-being of workers, his feeling reflects well on him because it shows that moral goods matter to him.

Particular states are virtuous or vicious, make one a morally better person, via a connection with moral concern. What, exactly, is the nature of this connection? It can be understood in causal terms; Ben's concern for social justice causes his particular feeling of moral indignation. Though my explanation of virtue and vice can be understood in purely causal terms, this can be misleading. A causal relation often implies a separation between the cause and effect; when a lightning strike causes a fire, first the lightning strike occurs and later the fire happens.[23] But this is not the case with someone's moral care and the particular mental states. Ben's concern for social justice doesn't stop when he feels indignant; it persists through the feeling.

Though virtuous states are caused by our moral concern, they also have a closer connection with it: manifestation. States manifest

23. An exception here is some conceptions of immanent causation, where cause and effect are not separate. See Zimmerman (1997) for an overview.

the underlying concern when they realize it in a certain domain; the particular state is an instantiation of the underlying concern. This is similar to other cases where an underlying orientation manifests as a particular event: Long-term racial tensions in a city manifest as a riot there. Someone's outgoing personality manifests as an excited back-and-forth at dinner. Someone's sense of style manifests as a particular stylish outfit. A comedian's humorous outlook on life manifests as a well-timed observation. Someone's underlying sexist outlook manifests as microagressions toward women.

In all of these cases the particular states are not merely the result of the underlying concern but a way in which it is realized. It is not as if there is one thing, the racial tensions, and another, the riot. The racial tension is present in the riot; this particular riot is a way that this tension manifests. The comedian's witty comment is not simply *the result* of her humorous outlook but a way that this outlook manifests in the conversational domain. Similarly, Ben's indignation over poor working conditions is not *merely* the result of his concern for justice but is also a *manifestation* of this concern. It is the way his underlying concern gets realized in the emotional realm. Particular states, such as emotions and pleasures, are not simply the result of what we care about but a way in which our cares manifest in our mental lives.

The account works the same way for vice, though it is slightly more complex. States can be vicious in two ways: by manifesting a lack of moral concern or by manifesting a morally bad concern. Someone can be a bad person by being indifferent to morality or by having a positive orientation to something morally bad. For example, being a neglectful father manifests a lack of concern for the well-being of one's child and so is vicious. Being a cruel father, however, is vicious by manifesting not only the absence of concern but a positive concern *to harm* one's child.

This also explains how *lacking* a mental state can be vicious—if my lack of indignation upon hearing of an unfair trial manifests a lack of concern for justice, then my lack of emotion reflects poorly on my moral character. This will be particularly relevant later on, when I distinguish morally significant emotional and attentional deficits from morally irrelevant ones (such as those associated with autism or attention-deficit disorder). Many states can be virtuous, even though lacking them is not always vicious. As we will see, this allows for cultural and personal diversity among virtuous people.

A FEW WORRIES

Weather Watchers and cases of locked-in syndrome show how one can be morally virtuous or vicious in a variety of ways that do not involve overt action. Seeing virtuous states as those that manifest moral concern best explains both how virtue is possible in these cases and what links the various types of states that can be virtuous or vicious. In what follows I respond to a few worries one might have about the account in a way that, hopefully, will clarify both its content and its scope.

What about Outer Virtue?

In focusing on inner virtues and vices, I hope to highlight the moral relevance of these states and correct the excessive focus on overt action in moral theory. I don't mean to give the impression that *all* virtues are inner virtues. Overt action is an important part of moral life; one of the primary challenges for all of us is how to come to behave in ways that we should.

These concerns, however, do not exhaust the domain of moral virtue. By thinking about beings like Weather Watchers and people with locked-in syndrome, we can come to see that the aspects of their moral character, aspects that don't depend on overt action, are aspects of our moral character, too. Our cares and concerns can manifest as inner states, as pleasure or emotion, and so are relevant to moral character.

What's So Good about Manifesting Moral Concern?

Imagine that moral concern happened to produce bright green freckles all over the body of those who possess it. In this world the more one cares about morality, the more green freckles one gets; people who are indifferent to moral goods are clear-skinned, while those who care very much have green spots all over. This might make sizing people up easier since having green freckles would be very good *evidence* that someone is a good person. We can even suppose that the freckles aren't merely symptoms of moral concern but a bodily manifestation of it. It is one part of the way that one's moral concern is realized physically.

And yet, though the freckles are manifestations of moral concern, there doesn't seem to be anything *good* about having green freckles. Parents in this world might object to their son marrying a woman without green freckles, but they need not think that the lack of freckles *itself* is bad. It's what the lack of freckles *reveals* that they're worried about; the freckles are just an indication of what really is bad.

Once again, the green freckles case can seem a bit far-fetched, but there are similar real-life cases: In a friendly card game, Susan is accused of cheating and blushes because she finds the idea of cheating so embarrassing. Jonathan watches a documentary about the Holocaust and, because of his concern for others, he is physically ill. There's nothing good about having the blood rush to your cheeks or being sick to your stomach, but if these states really do manifest moral concern, they seem virtuous—they reflect well on Susan and Jonathan, even though the states themselves are undesirable. Virtuous states say something about what kind of person their possessor is; this is compatible with a variety of other ways the state might be useful or useless, good or bad, and pleasant or unpleasant.

If things like blushing, nausea, emotions, or pleasures can be virtuous or vicious, then it might seem like we're praiseworthy or blameworthy for these states. It is important here to distinguish being morally virtuous or vicious from deserving praise or blame. It is possible for someone to be a worse person in certain ways, but not deserve blame for it. It is vicious when I am angry at the slow-moving line at the post office or when I feel pleasure at seeing someone I dislike fall down, but it is a distinct (and open) question whether or not I deserve *blame* in these cases.[24] If blame applies only to voluntary actions, I may be to blame for *acting* on such reactions, but the reactions *themselves* are not blameworthy. I will remain agnostic on these questions—it is important to keep in mind that such reactions can make me a morally worse person regardless of whether or not I deserve blame for them.

---

24. This is a hotly contested subject in moral theory. Some, like Scanlon (2008), take blame to be simply a negative character assessment, which seems to make blame and vice conceptual bedfellows. However, he also claims that blame in general has to do with action—that we blame someone *for* doing something. Robert Adams (1985) and George Sher (2006, 51ff.), however, argue that we rightly blame people for traits, like being ungrateful, or attitudes, like being racist.

Why Not Think Virtuous States Are Simply Those That Tend to Produce Good Effects?

Isn't a general connection to good effects enough for a state to be virtuous? Julia Driver offers an important defense of just such a view; for her, a trait is virtuous when it tends to produce good effects.[25] States that tend to product good effects are virtuous, and those that tend to produce bad effects are vicious.

Inner virtues can be understood as counterexamples to this claim. After all, they are states that reflect well on one's moral character, but since they are virtuous even when they do not manifest in overt action, they need not tend to produce any effects on others. Consider psychologically isolated and unexpressed feelings of schadenfreude or racial contempt. Because they are not of a type that produces any effects, they come out as neither virtuous nor vicious on Driver's account. But it does seem that a person would be morally better if they lacked such feelings, even though the feelings don't produce any effects.

There is, however, another reason to reject this view of virtue. On this view, the devil could make *any* mental state vicious simply by harming others any time someone experiences it. If the devil reliably caused mayhem any time people feel sympathy for the poor, then having sympathy for the poor would thereby be vicious. Suppose I were to donate to the NAACP every time my neighbor has a racist thought. I make his racist thoughts beneficial, but I haven't made them virtuous—they, for example, still don't seem to reflect well on him. More realistically, someone in the midst of a political revolution may well benefit others by becoming more ruthless and callous; having these traits may produce more

---

25. See Driver (2001).

overall good. But that does not make ruthlessness and callousness virtuous.[26]

Many traits may be good or useful by producing good consequences, but that does not make them virtuous. Suppose that squeamishness, laziness, or contempt turned out to, in general, produce better effects, say because people found immoral things gross or a hassle or low class. That might make those traits beneficial or useful, but it need not make them virtuous. Being lazy or contemptuous might be good in the sense that the world goes better, but those traits need not make those who have them morally better people. Something can be useful or beneficial without being virtuous.

There can even be a tension between these features. A doctor may help her patients more effectively if she cultivates an indifference to their suffering. Suppose a rich person adopts a policy of donating to effective charities every time people have a racist or sexist thought. On finding out about this, some people might then decide to cultivate such thoughts. The donations amount to much more than they could ever give themselves, so they take time out of each day to dwell in racist and sexist thoughts, encouraging them to flourish. If they really do this in order to produce the benefits of the donations, it's natural to describe them as engaging in a kind of moral martyrdom. They brings about good effects by making *themselves morally worse*; they help others at the cost of their own moral character.

Moral martyrs like this are difficult to evaluate overall; they bring about good effects, but only by cultivating a vicious state in themselves. Their *cultivation* can be virtuous; it does, after all, show moral concern. But that need not make the resulting state virtuous.

26. See Tessman (2005) for a denial of this claim.

Moreover, if we see virtues simply as traits that produce good effects, it becomes hard to describe the moral cost of this cultivation.

Why Isn't a Particular State Virtuous via Its Own Relation to Moral Goods?

One might now wonder: Why not simply call individual states virtuous or vicious based on how the *states themselves* relate to moral goods? This would simplify the account by eliminating underlying moral concern from the explanation. It can be tempting to think of states as being good in this way: Positive states, like pleasure or joy, are virtuous when directed toward moral goods and negative states, like displeasure or indignation, or when directed at morally bad things like injustice or cruelty. It is worth noting that it is compatible with my account of virtue that states can be morally good or important in just this way. Being good in this way, however, is not the same as being virtuous.

A state can fail to be virtuous despite aiming at a moral good by being disconnected from one's character. First let's consider an example of overt action: Someone who picks up litter purely out of pathological compulsion acts in a way that aims at the good. Insofar as the behavior is the result of a compulsion, it is disconnected from what she cares about; it doesn't say anything about her moral character in the same way that the urge to scratch an itch does not reflect on one's moral character. The behavior is good in that it aims at a genuinely valuable goal, but it doesn't say anything about the person's moral character. Though the action itself aims at something good (it's good for trash to be in a trash can), it doesn't say much about the character of the person who performs it.

The same can happen with inner states. Recall the example of scientists placing an implant in my brain. Suppose that the implant makes me feel displeasure and that the scientists reliably activate it when I notice something unjust. Since my displeasure is a negative reaction to something morally bad, there is something good about it. However, it doesn't say much about me—I might feel such displeasure from the implant and still care very little about injustice; after a while I may come to dislike injustice not because I care about others, but because it activates the implant and causes me displeasure. A god looking down from the heavens, charged with evaluating my moral character, would rightly think that the displeasure caused by the implant doesn't count in my favor. If asked, she could respond, "He doesn't *care* about those unfair raises at work; he just has one of those implants in his brain." These issues will be important in my discussion of how particular mental disorders like psychopathy, autism, obsessive-compulsive disorder, and attention-deficit disorder relate to one's moral character.

Can Anything At All Be a Virtue?

There is a way in which this account can seem to be too broad. If being virtuous is simply a matter of manifesting moral concern, then can't *anything at all* be a virtue? So if carrying boxes can manifest moral concern, should there be a virtue called box carrying? The account lacks the resources to produce a list of *the* virtues.[27]

This is true, but I find it to be a feature of the account rather than a defect. Virtue ethicists tend to be list makers. This often results in discussions about which virtues are on whose list and which virtues have been left out. Sometimes these illuminate genuine moral disagreements, but in many cases distinguishing virtues is a matter of taste—recall that Aristotle takes giving small gifts to be a different

27. Thanks to Derek Bowman and Dave Estlund for pressing me on these issues.

virtue from giving large ones. My account is compatible with a variety of ways of grouping virtuous states into virtues; they can be grouped by the domain (action, emotion, attention, etc), by their object, or by involving similar types of practices. I don't wish to commit myself to a single correct way of grouping states and actions into virtues, in part because I strongly suspect there isn't one. My aim is to show that there are natural patterns of virtuous *states* that do not require behavioral action.

The account does explain why certain kinds of states cannot be morally virtuous or vicious. States that do not (or cannot) manifest our cares and concerns cannot be virtuous or vicious. This explains why many kinds of states do not say anything about whether or not one is a good person. Sometimes it is because the state does not involve moral concern or a lack thereof; the pleasure of a cool breeze on a hot day or a preference for atonal music does not say anything about whether or not someone is a morally good person. The same is true of certain bodily traits like being tall, diabetic, or club-footed; these say nothing about one's moral character. I'll argue that this is also true of purely cognitive abilities like cleverness, the ability to do mental math, or having attention-deficit disorder.

Neo-Aristotelians may insist on calling some of these traits vicious (or, a favored euphemism, "defects"). It is true that such traits may prevent someone from fulfilling distinctively human functions and may involve living a less-than-perfectly-ideal human life. They are not, I will argue, vicious in the sense of making someone a morally worse person.

Many of these traits may be useful in moral development, but just because a trait is *useful* for becoming virtuous does not make the trait itself virtuous. For example, having supportive and nonabusive parents is *useful* for becoming a good person, but one is not a morally worse person simply because one has abusive parents. Similarly, being clever *can* help one to become a better person, but that doesn't mean a less clever person is a morally worse person.

CONCLUSION

An inability to act does not preclude having moral character, and this shows that some aspects of our moral lives are act-independent. The best explanation of this is to see virtuous states as manifestations of an underlying moral concern. This is why an account of virtue does not simply fall out of an account of right action; thinking about what it is to be a good person means thinking about more than actions and the mental states that go along with them.

Part of what makes this the best explanation is that it allows for various desirable pluralities within virtue. It offers a unifying explanation of how states in vastly different modalities can all be assessed as virtuous or vicious; what allows actions, emotions, thoughts, and pleasures to be virtuous is their connection with one's underlying moral orientation. It also allows for a plurality not only in the type of state but also within types. As I will argue in the case of emotions, it is possible for different emotions to be equally virtuous. If one person's indignation and another's sadness both manifest the same degree of moral concern, they are equally virtuous. This explains why we do not think of all the people we admire morally as having identical emotional lives. As we will see in detail, their emotional personalities can differ in ways that do not make them less virtuous.

In what follows, I hope to both clarify this account of virtue and defend substantive moral claims by discussing how particular types of inner states can be virtuous or vicious. So far, I've defended a thesis about virtuous and vicious states in general. However, thinking about how the account works when applied to particular kinds of inner states will illuminate various aspects both of the general account and of the moral status of the states themselves. In the following chapters, I will examine in more detail how this account works for pleasure, emotion, and attention.

Chapter 3

Pleasure

Peter experiences a warm sense of satisfaction whenever he learns one of his colleagues has been fired. When Laura reads about the plight of refugees, she finds that she feels a deeply visceral displeasure. The pleasure and displeasure experienced by Peter and Laura are not voluntary—being pleased or displeased is not something they *do*, but something that happens to them. These reactions need not motivate voluntary action either. Peter may never take any steps to get others fired or even express his enjoyment outwardly; the refugees that Laura reads about may have vanished hundreds of years ago. And yet these involuntary reactions themselves seem to say something about Peter and Laura: "What kind of person" Peter might think to himself on a particularly introspective night, "would feel *pleased* when a colleague is fired?" while Laura's friend might try to alleviate her uneasiness by telling her, "You feel that way because you're such a kind-hearted person."

Cases like those of Peter and Laura show that pleasure and displeasure *can* be relevant to moral character. Not all pleasure, however, is relevant to these evaluations. The pleasure we experience when tasting a fine Scotch or when our favorite team wins the championship need not say anything about our moral character. Nor does the displeasure we feel when the weather is too humid or when we stub a toe say much about our moral character.

There are various questions one might ask about the relevance of pleasure to moral character: Can morally good actions be motivated by pleasure? Should a virtuous person see pleasure as a reason for acting? Questions about the moral relevance of pleasure, however, need not be limited to its connection with overt action. Rather than take up these questions, in this chapter I will defend an account of how pleasure can be a virtuous or vicious state independently of any connection to overt actions.[1]

After a brief overview of what pleasure is, I will give a general account of when pleasure and displeasure are virtuous or vicious and why. In brief, I will argue that pleasures are relevant to moral character when they manifest moral concerns. I will then discuss the relationship between pleasure and concern in more detail and, in doing so, highlight some of the psychological complexities that arise.

Finally, I will use the account to solve some puzzles about virtuous and vicious pleasure by focusing on schadenfreude, pleasure in the suffering of others, and *mudita*, pleasure in the success and good fortune of others. First, I will argue that it explains why schadenfreude is generally vicious but also explains a variety of complexities associated with it. For example, how pleasure in the deserved suffering of others can be vicious and pleasure in the undeserved suffering of others can be virtuous. Next, I will argue that it also explains why *mudita*, a state emphasized in Buddhist ethics, is morally virtuous. In both cases, these states can be virtuous without appearing in overt actions.

---

1. I am here disagreeing with the letter but not, perhaps, the spirit of Aristotle when he says, "We must take as a sign of states of character the pleasure or pain that ensues on acts" (*NE* 1104b3). He is right that pleasure is relevant to moral character, but wrong to think that such pleasures and pains are limited to those that accompany action.

WHAT IS PLEASURE?

It is no easy task to give an account of what pleasure is. Part of the difficulty stems from the fact that there seem to be innumerable varieties: Pleasures can be gustatory, aesthetic, intellectual, sexual, spiritual, and social (to name just a few types). To complicate matters further, many pleasures have several of these aspects at once— the smell of a food your mother made you as a child can provide pleasure that is at once both gustatory and social. It can be difficult to tell what is common between enjoying a well-made espresso, an orgasm, and finally understanding a Japanese sentence.

First, a note about terminology. Because I will use the term "pleasure" to cover all of these cases, I will contrast it with "displeasure" rather than "pain." Though we often talk about emotional (or, less commonly, intellectual) pains, the paradigmatic sense of the term is physical and some physical pains can be pleasurable, for example, the pain of an intense workout or of particularly strong wasabi. In using the term "displeasure," however, I mean something stronger than the common-usage meaning, which is often closer to a cold sense of disapproval coupled with slight annoyance (as when a supervisor finds his employee's chronic lateness to be "displeasing"). In this sense I will ask the term to do more work than it usually does; though the term "displeasure" does not seem to capture the intensity of the negative reaction of learning that a friend has cancer, my use will include such reactions.

Overly technical definitions such as "experiences with a positively valenced qualitative aspect" seem to offer little more than saying "pleasures are experiences which are pleasant." I will not attempt to provide a complete account of pleasure itself here but will simply attempt to characterize the features of the sort of pleasure that is relevant to character evaluations. Most generally, I will take pleasure (and displeasure) to be a kind of occurrent, object-directed, conscious state.

It is occurrent in the sense that it has duration in time, with a beginning and an end; when I find some money on the sidewalk, I feel pleased for a while, but eventually it wears off. Of course, the duration can vary: The pleasure of a cool breeze lasts but a moment, while the pleasure of a promotion may last several weeks. Pleasure is a conscious state in the sense that it disappears when we fall into a coma or dreamless sleep.[2] It is something that we experience; it is characterized in part by how it feels to us. Like emotions, pleasures generally take an object. I am pleased *with* the delicious meal or displeased *with* my friend's rude behavior.[3] Although it seems possible to have objectless pleasure, perhaps when feeling a general sense of well-being, my discussion will focus on pleasure that takes an object.

None of these features of pleasure and displeasure will be essential to my account of the relevance to moral character. What is essential for my purposes is that pleasure and displeasure are involuntary, inner states. Feeling pleased or displeased is not an action; it is not something we *do*, but something that *happens to us*. We cannot simply feel pleased or displeased at will.

This is not to deny any link between pleasure and action. Pleasure and displeasure often cause us to behave in certain ways. You might leave a coffee shop because the music displeases you. You might order another drink at a bar because the conversation is so pleasant. We often act *in response* to pleasure or displeasure and act

---

2. See Schroeder (2004, 76).

3. Though pleasures and emotions share many features, pleasures are not themselves emotions. Though pleasure and displeasure are *elements* of emotions like joy, glee, misery, and sorrow, they are not the whole story of these emotions. The fact that certain emotions *are* pleasurable or displeasurable suggests that hedonic tone is not simply another emotion but a distinct feature that emotions can have. I thank Nomy Arpaly for helpful discussion of this issue.

with the goal of attaining pleasure in the future (or at least, avoiding displeasure!).

But pleasure and displeasure *itself* is distinct from these associated actions. We can, for example, act as if we are pleased when we really are not. Someone opening a gift that they absolutely hate may *act as if* they are pleased by the gift; they raise the tone and volume of their voice, force a smile, and say, "Wow, thanks! This is really great!" We can also feel pleasure or displeasure without revealing it—when dealt a great hand while playing poker or when dealing with a rude customer at work. Even though we experience pleasure over our straight flush and displeasure with the screaming customer, this experience need not be expressed in our external behavior. Though it is commonly associated with overt action, pleasure itself is an inner state distinct from such actions and can be relevant to one's moral character independently of such associations.

HEDONIC VIRTUE AND VICE

As we've seen, some pleasures and displeasures do not say much of anything about one's moral character. Some of these are physical: Taking pleasure in a cool breeze on a hot day or being displeased when stubbing a toe do not make us morally better or worse. Like hunger and thirst, they are simply part of the day-to-day operation of a normal, embodied human being. Other pleasures, like those of Peter and Laura, *do* seem to make one a morally better or worse person. What explains the difference?

It can be tempting to think that physical pleasure or displeasure cannot be virtuous or vicious. And yet Laura's displeasure when reading about the plight of the refugees does have physical aspects: a tightness in her chest and shaking, clammy hands. This kind of psychosomatic displeasure is different from the simple pain of stubbing a toe. Though both are very real physical responses, Laura's displeasure is rooted in her mental life in an important way; the genesis of her physical pain is mental displeasure. Someone who is nauseous because of their mental anguish at seeing photographs of concentration camps is importantly different from someone who is nauseous simply because they ate rotten food.

At the other extreme, there are also purely intellectual pleasures that can be irrelevant to one's moral character. Under most circumstances, taking pleasure in the interplay of shapes in an abstract painting, the form of a geometry proof, or the syncopated rhythms in a drum solo do not say anything about one's moral character.[4] What, then, differentiates pleasures that can make one a morally better or worse person from ones that cannot?

Pleasure and displeasure reflect on our moral character when they are manifestations of morally important cares or concerns. The pleasure of a cool breeze on a hot day and the displeasure of stubbing a toe do not manifest any of our morally relevant cares or concerns. Peter's pleasure at his colleague's misfortune, however, seems to manifest at least a *lack* of concern for his colleague's well-being. Laura's displeasure at reading about refugees seems to manifest a concern for their rights and well-being. Peter and Laura's pleasure is morally relevant because it manifests something about their concern for the well-being of others, a fundamental moral concern.

Consider some evidence that the underlying concern determines whether or not pleasure is morally virtuous: Our evaluation

---

4. Compare with Adams (2006, 20–21), who considers bad aesthetic taste to be a minor moral vice. I take it for granted that aesthetic vices are not always moral vices. Having bad taste might make you unrefined, but it does not make you a morally bad person; feeling more pleasure when viewing a Thomas Kinkade painting than that of a Dutch master might make one a philistine, but it does not make one *morally* worse.

of how pleasure or displeasure reflects on someone's moral character changes when we get information about the underlying concern. The Chinese philosopher Mengzi describes the displeasure a gentleman experiences when confronted with animal slaughter: "As for the relation of gentlemen to birds and beasts, if they see them living, they cannot bear to see them die." When I read this, I'm apt to think that the displeasure of the gentleman in question reflects pretty well on his moral character. After all, he probably can't bear to see animals slaughtered because he cares about their well-being.

Things change, however, when Mengzi continues: "If they hear their cries, they cannot bear to eat their flesh. Hence, gentlemen keep their distance from the kitchen."[5] Now the gentleman does not seem to be such a good person after all. His conclusion reveals that what he cares about is not so much the suffering of the *animals*, but *his own appetite* and *his own displeasure*. What changed after reading that final sentence was not anything about the displeasure that I thought the gentleman experienced or the object of this displeasure, but what kinds of concerns I took it to manifest.

As we will see in detail, similar hedonic responses can manifest different concerns: Consider two people who both become nauseous after seeing photos of concentration camps. One feels nausea because they have a general squeamishness and "can't stand the sight of blood," while the other feels it because they find the reality of how human beings have in fact treated other human beings to be deeply abhorrent. Both experience physical pain as the result of mental displeasure, but that of the latter is relevant to moral character while that of the former is not.

The relevant concern necessary for pleasure to be virtuous or vicious need not be for a specific outcome. Though he was

5. *Mengzi* 1A7.

pleased when his colleague was fired, Peter may not have had a *specific* concern for *this particular* colleague's termination. It may have been something more general; he may have cared about something bad happening to "those jerks in accounting" or simply that "one of those button-down East Coast guys gets the wind taken out of his sails."

Pleasure and displeasure, then, are virtuous or vicious via the cares and concerns they manifest. The devil, as usual, is in the details, and more must be said both about the nature of pleasure and its connection with our cares and concerns.

PLEASURE AND CONCERN

There are, in general, strong connections between our concerns and our pleasure; caring about something *generally* produces pleasure and displeasure regarding it, and a lack of concern for something usually results in a lack of such pleasure and displeasure. If I don't care about baseball, I will typically not be particularly pleased to see it on TV nor will I be displeased to hear that the players have gone on strike. If I care deeply about abstract art, then I will likely be pleased to learn of a Frank Stella exhibit in my city and feel displeasure when I discover it has been cancelled.

This also applies to moral cases. If someone does not care about the rights of women, they are not likely to be displeased when such rights are violated or be pleased when they are upheld. Someone who cares deeply about the homeless will likely be pleased to learn that a new shelter has opened and displeased to see policies that harm them passed by local government.

I use phrases like "likely" and "usually" here because these connections are not necessary connections but contingent facts about the mental lives of humans *in general*. I may, for example, care a great deal about abstract art but fail to feel pleasure upon hearing of the exhibit because I am exhausted from lack of sleep or under the influence of a sedative. Pleasure and displeasure *can* reflect on our moral character, and when they do, it is because we feel (or fail to feel) them in virtue of our cares or concerns. Many things can sever the link between my concerns and my hedonic state. If I fail to feel displeasure at the unfair treatment of a female colleague because I am sick, exhausted, or it is my first day on a new sedative, it does not reflect on my moral character.

Despite cases like these, experiencing pleasure and displeasure *is* intimately connected with our cares and concerns. This is implicit in a common decision-making aid. When faced with two options, say two very good restaurants, we can sometimes find ourselves unable to decide between them. In these situations it can be helpful to flip a coin: "Heads Italian, tails Japanese." The purpose of the coin-flip is not, however, to give a verdict but instead to provide insight: We see how the coin lands and notice whether or not we are pleased with the outcome. Do we feel pleased ("Oh good! It's heads") or displeased ("Damn. Well, I *guess* Italian is okay")? The reason this method can work is that our pleasure or displeasure at the outcome is reliable evidence of what we care about. We might learn that we do care about having Italian or that it doesn't matter much either way.[6]

This phenomenon is also at the heart of many instances of self-discovery. A new professor who thinks of himself as completely research focused might discover that he *does* care about teaching after experiencing unexpected displeasure when reading through a stack of negative teaching evaluations. A doctor might discover that she does not care about professional awards after all when failing to

---

6. This decision procedure is also discussed in Lycan (1988, 58) and Schroeder (2004, 74).

feel pleased after learning that she has received an important award in her field.

It is critical to appreciate that the cares and concerns that underlie pleasure are often varied and very difficult to distinguish. Consider the moral assessment of those who experience pleasure over the death of vicious people. When Osama Bin Laden was killed, many people in America experienced great pleasure and celebrated wildly. This spurred much public debate about whether or not it is morally acceptable to take pleasure in and celebrate a death. Much of this debate focused on the practical consequences of celebration, such as whether or not it would make future terrorist attacks more likely.

These celebrations raised another question: Aside from practical concerns about celebration, is it vicious to take pleasure, even inwardly, in someone's death? Not all who were pleased by the event seemed equally virtuous or vicious—whether or not taking pleasure in the death of Bin Laden was virtuous or vicious depended on which concerns such pleasure manifested. It mattered, for example, whether or not one was pleased with the event *despite* the fact that it was a death, without regard for the element of death, or *because* it was a death.

Pleasure at Bin Laden's death manifested a wide variety of cares and concerns in different people. For some, the pleasure simply manifested a concern for people to be cheerful and party: One celebrator told the *New York Observer*, "It's weird to celebrate someone's death. It's not exactly what we're here to celebrate, but it's wonderful that people are happy."[7] This doesn't seem particularly vicious; if this person is to count as vicious at all, it is because of a lack of concern for the fact that the occasion of this particular party *was* someone's death.

7. Weeks (2011).

The pleasure of others manifested concerns that resist simple evaluation. For example, someone concerned for patriotism *über alles*, happy simply that *"we"* came out on top. Others still may have simply been adventure seekers, caring about the details of an exciting combat mission. Such pleasures count as vicious for manifesting limited and parochial concerns (as if non-American deaths "don't count") or a lack of concern for the moral weight of killing someone (as if adventure is more important than human life). As positive concerns, however, these are not as vicious as someone who maliciously loves seeing casualties of war or someone who wishes for an increase in religious animosity.

Other positive concerns seemed to many to be less vicious; the philosopher of law Brian Leiter described to *Time* magazine the "emotional cleansing when the wrongdoers get what they deserve."[8] Many, like Leiter, saw nothing wrong with pleasure at Bin Laden's death as long as it was not simply *as* death, but rather *as* comeuppance. For them, such pleasure isn't vicious because one doesn't want just *any* old witch to be killed, but only *the wicked one*. Those who accept retributive justice as good will see pleasure that manifests a concern for retribution as virtuous, while those who see retribution as morally bad will see such pleasure as vicious. The virtuous or viciousness of pleasure that manifests a concern for retribution depends on whether or not retribution itself is morally good.[9]

Even less controversial are those whose pleasure manifested a concern for their own safety and the safety of others. This is the pleasure we experience when the hurricane is over. This pleasure

---

8. Kluger (2011).
9. There are, as usual, further complexities here. One who accepts retributive justice may still think pleasure in a just killing to be vicious. See my discussion of Julia Driver's happy executioner later.

seems not only less vicious than the pleasures described earlier but is perhaps even virtuous. Pleasure at Bin Laden's death only because one takes the danger to innocent lives to be lessened seems to reflect well on the person who experiences it. This is because the concerns the pleasure manifests are morally good—a concern for one's own safety and the safety of others.

Though those celebrating Bin Laden's death all took pleasure in the same event, the underlying concerns were very different. In practice, these various concerns are difficult to distinguish and often come packaged together—the real-life people who celebrated the death of Bin Laden likely had a combination of concerns for safety, for retribution, *and* for an occasion to have a party. The lack of isolated cares or concerns is not a problem for the account; one is virtuous *to the extent* that their pleasure manifests morally good cares and concerns. These cares and concerns can be difficult, if not impossible, for us to know simply by observing those expressing pleasure. This is why we should not be too quick to judge an entire crowd in a video as virtuous or vicious.

It what follows, I will show how this account can best explain cases where our pleasure in the fortunes and misfortunes of others reflects on our moral character. Such cases are not determined by what one deserves but instead by the underlying concerns that such pleasures manifest.

SCHADENFREUDE: SUFFERING AND DESERT

Of pleasures taken to be relevant to moral character, the one that has received the most ink in the Western philosophical literature is schadenfreude, pleasure at another's misfortune. Though the German term can refer to a more robust and complex emotional response, here I will use it to mean pleasure in another's misfortune. Arthur Schopenhauer gives one of the strongest condemnations of it:

> In some respects the opposite of envy is the *malicious joy at the misfortunes of others* [schadenfreude]. Yet to feel envy is human; but to indulge in such malicious joy is fiendish and diabolical. There is no more infallible sign of a thoroughly bad heart and profound moral worthlessness than an inclination to a sheer and undisguised malignant joy of this kind.[10]

Such a blanket condemnation of *all* pleasure in the suffering of others has struck many as too strong. One response is to point out that misfortunes and sufferings come in degrees, so it can seem to be a stretch to call pleasure in trivial sufferings morally vicious. After all, is it really *vicious* to take pleasure in inconsequential sufferings?[11]

It is important, however, to remember that moral vice also comes in degrees. It is not a *serious* vice for me to feel a pleasant sense of satisfaction when I see my friend in a frustrating struggle to get his key to open the rusty lock or when I see that traffic going the opposite direction on the highway is at a complete standstill. Assuming that my pleasure in these cases is actually at the misfortunes of others and not, say, the absurdity of modern life, those who take all schadenfreude to be vicious need not say that I have a *major* moral vice. They can simply claim that my pleasure at these minor misfortunes constitutes a minor moral vice. Minor, yes, but still moral. Taking pleasure in these minor misfortunes need not make me a *bad* person, but I might be a *slightly morally better* person if I didn't delight in the everyday setbacks of others.

10. Schopenhauer (1840/1995, 135).
11. This objection is raised in Portmann (2000, 81ff.).

A more common response to the idea that *all* pleasure in the suffering of others is vicious is to claim that its viciousness depends on whether or not the misfortune is *deserved*. After all, if Peter's colleague really "had it coming," then it need not be vicious for Peter to feel pleased at the firing, even though it is a misfortune for the colleague.[12] On this view, a misfortune's being undeserved, or at least there being good evidence that it is undeserved, explains why taking pleasure in it is vicious. This claim stems from the idea that the heart of what makes schadenfreude vicious is a lack of concern for what is deserved.[13]

Though the moral status of schadenfreude does stem from the concerns it manifests, these concerns are *not* limited to what someone deserves. In what follows, I will argue that pleasure in *undeserved* suffering can be virtuous, and pleasure in *deserved* suffering can be vicious. Much of my discussion, particularly on pleasure in deserved sufferings, will assume that at least *some* sufferings or misfortunes *can* be deserved. Though it can be appealing to think that no one ever deserves to suffer, we need something to capture the difference between the firing of a diligent and committed teacher and that of one who has nothing but contempt for their job and students. There is an important way in which the firing of the latter is at least *more* warranted or justified than the firing of the former. Again, though parts of my discussion will assume that sufferings and misfortunes can be deserved, facts about whether or not a misfortune is

---

12. Aaron Ben-Ze'ev states this most clearly: "Pleasure whose object is undeserved misfortune must be considered morally unacceptable. It is ethically wrong to take pleasure in the undeserved misfortunes of others. However, when the misfortune is deserved, being pleased about this is not necessarily a vice" (2000, 375). See also Portmann (2000, 116).

13. For example, John Portmann writes, "*Schadenfreude* indicates something about how a person views justice and moral triviality" (2000, 116). Ben-Ze'ev agrees, "The important role deservingness plays in pleasure-in-others'-misfortune implies that this emotion can be found only in people who are sensitive to moral considerations" (2000, 376).

deserved do not settle the question of whether or not taking pleasure in it is virtuous or vicious.

Part of the reason for this stems from the nature of pleasure itself. Pleasure is rarely simply pleasure in an object, but more often in an object *as something*. This becomes clear when we think of cases where we agree with someone on the object of pleasure but disagree on the respect in which it is pleasing. A colleague and I might both take the same coffee to be pleasurable, though for him it is pleasing *as a source of caffeine* and for me it is pleasing *as a taste experience*. Getting the object right is not enough to make pleasure virtuous; we must also be pleased in the right way. If Geoff is displeased by torture only because torture displeases his girlfriend and he hates for his girlfriend to be displeased, Geoff is displeased by the right thing, but in the wrong way, and so is not a better person for it.[14]

In the background will be idea that considerations of what is *deserved* are not the only kind of morally relevant considerations. Consider, as Nomy Arpaly has pointed out, how our judgments about *what people deserve* and *what they should be given* can come apart. Often, virtuous people are pleased by the latter rather than the former. For example, the board of a company might think the CEO *deserves* a modest salary but also think that she *should be given* a very high salary so that she will not leave for another company. As a stockholder, I am apt to be pleased that she got the high salary, even though I do not think she deserves it. Arpaly offers other intuitive examples of this in the moral domain: One might think that a despot who tortured many people *deserves* to be tortured himself, but think that what he should be given is a life sentence. One might

---

14. Aristotle (*NE* 1118a32–4) offers the vivid example of a gourmand who only enjoys the bare physical contact with food and so wishes he had a very long throat. More recently, Arpaly (2004, 71) offers a similar example of someone who takes pleasure in reading *Lolita* as scandal rather than as literature.

think that everyone who drives with an open container of alcohol should be punished, but not think that everyone *deserves* such a punishment.[15]

There are also similar cases regarding benefits—a teacher might rightly judge that a student's work deserves unstinting praise but also wisely judge that he should be given only mild praise because anything more would go to the student's head and ruin his work ethic. Again in this case, the virtuous person would feel pleasure if the student does *not* get the praise he deserves and displeasure if he does; after all, it is not what is best for him.

VIRTUOUS PLEASURE IN UNDESERVED SUFFERING

A virtuous person can feel pleased that a student is denied deserved praise, because such pleasure manifests a concern for what is best for the student (or, less paternalistically, what will best help the student to promote his own ends). In a similar way, there can be virtuous pleasure in undeserved suffering. Pleasure in undeserved suffering *only as undeserved suffering* is vicious. It manifests a lack of concern for both well-being and justice. This is the charitable way to understand Schopenhauer's condemnation of schadenfreude: What is vicious is not taking pleasure in another's misfortune, but taking pleasure in it *only as an undeserved misfortune.*

There are, however, other ways to take pleasure in undeserved suffering: One can take pleasure in an undeserved misfortune of another as beneficial overall or in the long term, as better than the alternative, or as meaningful for some larger goal or purpose.

15. See Arpaly (1999, 51ff.).

Despite being cases where one takes pleasure in undeserved suffering, they need not be vicious and can even be virtuous.

Sometimes we are pleased at an undeserved misfortune because we see it as providing an opportunity for the future. If Peter knows that his colleague was a good worker and did not deserve to be fired, he may be pleased because he knows it will allow him to spend much needed time with his family and is the opportunity he needs to ultimately land a better job. Peter might take this misfortune to be the catalyst that pushes his colleague to strike out on his own, a chance he would not otherwise have taken.

The fact that these things might result from the firing does not mean that the firing itself is not a genuine misfortune; it is, after all, quite painful to go through. When Peter's pleasure is described in this way, however, it does not seem to reflect poorly on his moral character. He genuinely cares about his colleague and though he knows the firing is an undeserved misfortune, he is pleased in it not as such, but as beneficial in the long run. Peter need not deny that the event that pleases him is an instance of undeserved suffering to avoid being vicious, he can simply point out that the firing pleases him as an opportunity for future benefits for his colleague.

Another common situation in which pleasure in undeserved suffering can be virtuous is in cases of unavoidable harms. In some tragic situations, we feel pleasure at an undeserved misfortune as avoiding a worse result. Imagine you live in a town under the thumb of a ruthless gang. This gang occasionally engages in violent shows of force; they show up at a house chosen at random and publicly execute its owner. This is done both to maintain an atmosphere of fear and for their own amusement. Suppose that your neighbor has been selected for one of these visits and is dragged out of his house to be killed. At the last minute, however, they change their minds and instead simply punch him and take the cash he has on him.

Despite the fact that your neighbor did not deserve to be dragged out of his house and robbed, you may feel pleased at this outcome. Again, your pleasure is not in the event as an instance of undeserved suffering, but as better than the alternative. Of course, you'd be most pleased if he had been left alone, but under the circumstances you can be pleased that he was *merely* harassed and robbed. Your pleasure in this manifests concern for your neighbor despite being pleasure in an undeserved misfortune.

This can also happen in cases involving euthanasia. Suppose someone has the option of continued life at severely reduced quality or having their death hurried along (either passively or actively, it does not matter for my purposes). Whatever one's stance on the moral status of euthanasia, one is apt to feel pleased when what they take to be the better of the two misfortunes occurs. A supporter of euthanasia might think to herself, "Dad didn't deserve to die this way, but I'm pleased that he didn't have to linger in pain," while an opponent might reflect, "Mom doesn't deserve to suffer this way, but I'm pleased that she will die with dignity." In either case, one feels pleasure in an undeserved misfortune, not as such, but as better than the alternative.

Finally, some take pleasure in undeserved suffering as forwarding a higher goal or to be symbolic of that goal. Martyrs, by definition, suffer terrible misfortunes that they do not deserve, but do so for the sake of some larger cause. It is this feature that leads some to feel a kind of celebratory pleasure when contemplating such figures.

Consider Nicola Sacco and Bartolomeo Vanzetti, Italian immigrants to America who were unjustly executed in 1927 after an infamously corrupt trial. Many songs about this incident have an undeniably celebratory tone, particularly when focusing on the increased awareness of important issues (in this case, the treatment of immigrants) and the strength of character that suffering such undeserved misfortunes manifested. Woodie Guthrie, for example, celebrates them as exemplars, offering the refrain, "I'll remember these two good men/That died to show me how to live." Joan Baez sings of the two Italians, "The last and final moment is yours/That agony is your triumph."[16] The implication is that the agony they experienced is undeserved but also a political and symbolic triumph deserving of awed pleasure, having an important meaning in a larger context. These verses have a celebratory tone about an undeserved misfortune, not as suffering itself, but as a role in a larger cause.[17] There can be something triumphant about some undeserved agony, particularly when faced bravely, and pleasure in such triumph need not reflect poorly on those who experience it.

It is important to keep in mind here that one can take pleasure in an event and still wish that the event had not occurred. One can take pleasure in an act of bravery in battle, while still wishing that there had been no war at all (and so no battle and no brave act). One can take pleasure in a friend learning to walk again after a serious accident while wishing that the accident, and so her recovery, had never happened. Similarly, one can take pleasure in the undeserved suffering of Sacco and Vanzetti as a meaningful and beneficial

---

16. The songs are entitled "Two Good Men" and "Here's to You," respectively.

17. This is common in religious contexts, too. Judith Perkins (1995) discusses how martyr-dom was central to how early Christians saw themselves as suffering for an important cause, leading some to "embrace death" (40). Of course, they did not embrace just *any* death but death *as part of a meaningful spiritual struggle*. In contemporary Catholicism, one celebrates Christ's suffering on the cross, for example, by going over in detail the Stations of the Cross. This need not be celebration of suffering as such but of suffering *as playing a key soteriological role*.

political event *and* still think it would be better if they had never been executed.

As I will soon discuss, a virtuous person will probably not feel *only* pleasure in these situations. Nevertheless, this kind of celebratory pleasure in undeserved suffering is not vicious and can be virtuous if it manifests a concern for moral goods like justice, salvation, or even the inspiring character such suffering reveals. This can also happen on a less dramatic scale, too. We often experience pleasure in undeserved suffering *as* an occasion for valuable bonding or *as* a way to build character. Of course, this will often be tempered by displeasure in the suffering (more on such mixed states later), but insofar as the pleasure manifests moral concern, it will be virtuous.

These cases each involve their own complexities, but together they serve as counterexamples not only to those who take *all* pleasure in another's misfortune to be categorically vicious but also to those who take whether or not a misfortune is deserved to be sufficient for pleasure in it to count as vicious. There are a variety of ways to take pleasure in an undeserved misfortune that are not vicious and that can even be virtuous.

VICIOUS PLEASURE IN DESERVED SUFFERING

The story so far has been that pleasure in an undeserved suffering can fail to be vicious as long as it is not pleasant *as undeserved suffering* but rather *as something else*. As long as the "something else" is morally good, the pleasure doesn't reflect poorly on one's character. And yet there is a problem when it comes to deserved suffering. The problem is that such pleasure still seems vicious even when it is pleasure *as what is deserved*. An example by Julia Driver helps to sharpen this:

Consider the happy executioner, and our suspicions of such a character. A happy executioner enjoys his job; he loves the feel of the rope slithering though his fingers as he fashions a noose, he loves to hear the snap of the neck bones breaking, etc. Most believers in capital punishment also think that it is good for people to enjoy their work. Why then the repugnance toward the happy executioner?[18]

Driver is right that *something* seems amiss in the executioner's character, but what? Even if we stipulate that *all* of his executions are just, that is, they are deserved, something still seems unsavory about the executioner. Despite the fact that the misfortunes are, by stipulation, deserved, taking pleasure in them *as justice* still reflects poorly on his character. Why is this?

Driver's answer appeals to a claim about the nature of our pleasures. For her, human pleasure cannot be narrow enough to simply be pleasure in executions that are just. Our repugnance at the executioner's pleasure, then, is "Because [we] know that, given human nature, there is a distinct possibility that this chap's pleasures are not restricted to the punishment of vicious criminals." On this view, it is simply psychologically implausible that our hangman enjoys *only* deserved executions.

There is, however, reason to doubt the idea that human pleasure must be broad in this way. Reflection on our own pleasures reveals that they are often quite narrow. Consider, for example, my enjoyment of a family gathering. I might tell a friend that I generally enjoy family gatherings, except of course, if Uncle Max comes, in which case I am miserable. If Uncle Max brings his wife, however, it is enjoyable since he is less contrarian around her. If she is in a bad

18. This quote and the following one are from Driver (1996, 120–121).

mood, though, it is not enjoyable at all. But if the gathering is held outdoors, the attendance doesn't matter so much, unless of course it is raining or chilly. I would have little trouble going on like this for some time, and the longer I go on, the more it seems as though my pleasures in family gatherings are actually *very* narrow.

Another way to see this is to imagine you are confronted with a wish-granting genie. Knowing that this genie is a trickster, you try to be as careful as possible when describing what would please you. But no matter how careful you are, the genie will always conjure up something that fits *the letter* of the description you give but which in fact displeases you. In such a situation, your pleasures do not seem broad at all but *very* narrow; this is why articulating your wish is so difficult. "I wish I was married to Francesca," you say. But then you must continue, "but I don't want her to be disfigured, and I don't want us both turned into ducks, and I don't want her to be bullied into it by her father, and I don't want one or both of us in a coma, and I want the marriage to be happy and . . ." The longer you go on, the more it looks like what you take pleasure in is quite narrow after all.

Even if our pleasures can be narrow in the way that I've suggested, however, the problem remains. Suppose we stipulate that our happy executioner *does* have a very narrow pleasure—he only enjoys hangings that are deserved. He loves to hear the sound of *criminals' necks* snapping and the heavy breathing *of criminals* as they anticipate the drop. His pleasure in the deserved sufferings he inflicts seems to reflect poorly on his character *even if* his pleasures are narrow and only apply to *deserved* suffering.

Consider a similar case from Catholic theology regarding the pleasure that the saints in heaven have toward the suffering of sinners in hell. Aquinas in the *Summa* (in)famously claimed that the saints in heaven *do* take pleasure in the suffering of the sinners in hell. Presumably, if saints in heaven have any pleasure in the suffering of sinners, it is very narrow (they are, after all, *saints*). It also seems that if God doles out punishment, such punishment is deserved. And yet even Aquinas thinks that the pleasure the saints experience is in need of some explanation—something seems fishy about the idea that saints might *enjoy* suffering, even deserved suffering. Aquinas' solution is similar to the one discussed earlier: Though the saints enjoy the suffering of sinners, they enjoy it *in the right way.* The saints, he claims, enjoy the suffering of sinners *as justice* and so the suffering *itself* is merely the indirect cause of their joy.[19]

This solution doesn't seem to work. Even if the saints only take pleasure in the suffering of those in hell *as justice*, something seems amiss. Even if the happy executioner really does take pleasure in his job *as justice*, something still seems vicious about him. Narrowing the scope of the pleasure does not eliminate the sense that there is still something vicious about these characters. The answer, I think, lies in the fact that the situations of the saints and the executioner call for *both* pleasure *and* displeasure, and lacking one likely manifests a lack of moral concern in some other respect.[20]

MIXED HEDONIC STATES

It can be tempting to think of pleasure and displeasure as, like hot and cold, driving each other out.[21] This may be true of our overall hedonic state; one that sums together all the pleasure and displeasure we feel to give a net value for how pleased we are in total. This does not, however, mean that we cannot take both pleasure and

---

19. *Summa Theologica*, Question 94, Article 1–3.
20. Hurka (2001, 194ff.) explains how vindictiveness, the desire that a vicious person suffer deserved suffering, can be vicious on similar grounds.
21. See Schroeder (2004, 72) for one such description.

displeasure in the same object at the same time, albeit in different respects.

Imagine Catherine, who is in financial dire straits and unable to properly provide for her children. Now suppose that Catherine's father, with whom she was quite close, has died and left her a sizable inheritance. To simply ask, "Should Catherine be pleased or displeased at her father's death?" is to ask an incomplete question. Though there is an overall hedonic description of her state, supposing that she is not in a stake of shock, we expect this overall state to include *both* pleasure *and* displeasure. She will be pleased with it *as a financial event* allowing her to provide for her children, and displeased with it *as a personal loss.*

This is the key to what strikes us as vicious about the happy executioner and the saints who rejoice at the suffering of those in hell. These cases mention only the pleasure in the punishments *as justice.* And yet these events are also instances of great suffering and, as such, also warrant displeasure. It is not vicious for Catherine to be pleased with her father's death as a financial event, but it *is* vicious for her to feel *only* this pleasure and not also feel displeasure as a personal loss.[22]

Just as we expect a reflective and sensitive person to feel both pleasure and displeasure at these events, we expect a morally sensitive executioner or saint to feel both pleasure in the event as justice *and* displeasure in it as suffering. What is unnerving about the happy executioner is not his pleasure in executions as justice, but his *lack of displeasure* in them as suffering. Insofar as his lack of displeasure manifests a lack of concern for suffering, he is vicious.

22. See also Hurka (2001, 196), who says that undeserved pleasure warrants a mixed state because it's good as pleasure and bad as undeserved. My view is similar but rather than focus on what is warranted, what matters is the concerns that are manifested by the mixed hedonic state.

Looking only at a person's overall hedonic state can be misleading. Suppose that Catherine's sister experiences more overall displeasure from her father's death than Catherine. This might be because she cares about her father more deeply, or it could be that she cares very little about her financial responsibilities. Similarly, the happy executioner might be pleased overall because he is displeased with suffering but also is very pleased by justice, or he might be pleased overall because he derives the normal amount of pleasure from justice but is not displeased at all by suffering. This is an important difference not captured by considering only his overall level of pleasure.

PROPORTION AND VIRTUOUS PLEASURE

Let's suppose that the happy executioner cares about both the suffering of those he executes, which manifests as displeasure, *and* about justice, which manifests as pleasure. As it happens, he cares *very, very much* about justice and so finds his job to be *very* pleasant overall. There is nothing vicious about the concerns that his pleasure and displeasure manifest, and yet his pleasure in his work still seems to reflect poorly on him somehow. Does he care *too much* about justice? Though he cares about suffering as much as a normal person, is it somehow too little?

It is tempting to think that the intensity of virtuous pleasures (or displeasures) must be proportionate to the goodness (or badness) of their object.[23] It is natural to think that a good person will

---

23. Hurka (2001, 83ff.), for example, claims that it is vicious (in his terminology "intrinsically evil") to love something out of proportion to its value. For him, pleasure is explicitly included within the scope of his somewhat technical use of "loving"—he writes that "One can love *x* by desiring or wishing for it when it does not obtain, or by taking pleasure in it when it does obtain" (2001, 13).

take greater pleasure in better things and less pleasure in worse things: We should feel more pleased when a friend finds a hundred-dollar bill than when they find a five-dollar bill. We should feel more displeasure when someone loses a child than when they lose a pen.

The idea that the intensity of pleasures must be proportionate to their objects is true *if* the intensity of pleasure correlates with our level of concern. However, many factors other than our concern affect the intensity of our pleasure and displeasure, and many of them are morally irrelevant. Because of these psychological facts about the nature of pleasure, what really must be proportionate is the underlying *concern* that the pleasure manifests.

For example, the intensity of our pleasure is often changed by our expectations. Recall the role our expectations play in cases where we are pleased at the lesser of two misfortunes. If we expect a normal day, then we are likely to experience displeasure if our neighbor is robbed. If we expect that our neighbor will be murdered, however, we will feel pleasure when he is merely robbed. More general personality traits can affect this too: Optimists and pessimists can experience different degrees of pleasure at an event not because they have different degrees of *concern*, but because they have vastly different *expectations*.

The intensity of our pleasures and displeasures is also affected by situational factors about what we are used to. Consider a story from Dale Carnegie's *How to Win Friends and Influence People* in which a salesman, Sid Levy, makes a call on a customer whose name is particularly difficult to pronounce:

> When I greeted him by his full name: "Good afternoon, Mr. Nicodemus Papadoulos," he was shocked. For what seemed like several minutes there was no reply from him at all. Finally, he said with tears rolling down his cheeks, "Mr. Levy, in all the

fifteen years I have been in this country, nobody has ever made the effort to call me by my right name."[24]

For most of us, being called by our right names does not result in much pleasure. If we are used to hearing people mispronounce it, however, we are likely to experience much more pleasure at hearing it pronounced correctly. This doesn't mean that the rest of us *care* about the correct pronunciation of our names less than Nicodemus, but we do take less pleasure in it because we are used to hearing our names pronounced correctly.

A resident of a country with frequent power cuts is likely to be very pleased when they flip a light switch and the lights actually come on, whereas an average first-world resident is unlikely to experience much pleasure at all. This does not mean that the first-world person cares about electricity less or is less concerned with having power; they are, after all, quite upset on the rare occasions when they do lose power. They experience less pleasure at the lights coming on not because they care less, but simply because they are accustomed to it.

What we are used to can also change fairly quickly. Nicodemus's pleasure at hearing the correct pronunciation of his name could decrease or even disappear after a few weeks if everyone he knows started saying it properly. His pleasure would decrease not because he started to care any less about it, but simply by getting used to it. After a few days of returning to a country with stable electricity, the former third-world resident's delight in flipping a switch and having the lights actually come on will likely fade.

Returning to the happy executioner, what seems unnerving is that, without other information about his situation or psychology,

24. Carnegie (1936/1981, 77).

his disproportionate pleasure suggests a vicious disproportionate *concern*. If he really does care about both suffering and justice but is pleased because he cares *a lot* about justice, his pleasure is vicious because it manifests a disproportionate concern for justice. A good person would care as much about the justice as about the suffering, and if his pleasure manifests his concern, he cares too little about the suffering he inflicts.

This is clear in the case of the saints taking pleasure in the suffering of sinners in hell. If we suppose that they care both about justice and about people not suffering, without any further psychological or situational explanation of why their pleasure in justice is so intense, it suggests a lack of concern for the well-being of others. After all, if they really do care about both justice and people avoiding suffering, they would also be *very* displeased to see many, *many* people suffering *unimaginable* tortures.[25]

MUDITA: SYMPATHETIC PLEASURE

The lion's share of discussion of pleasures directed toward others in the Western philosophical literature has focused on schadenfreude. In Buddhist work on ethics, however, there is much discussion of virtuous pleasure in the good fortune of others—*mudita*. Often translated as "sympathetic joy," it is, like schadenfreude, a complex response involving pleasure, the emotions, and attention. However, my discussion here will focus only on the hedonic aspect of this response—taking pleasure in the success and good fortune of others.

---

25. Aquinas denies this too; he argues that the saints cannot pity the suffering of those in hell because those in heaven cannot share in any unhappiness (*Summa* Q.94 A.2). See also the discussion in Hurka (2001, 195).

A good place to start is the fifth-century Indian philosopher Buddhaghosa's instructions on developing *mudita*:

> Or on seeing or hearing about a dear person being happy, cheerful and glad, *mudita* can be aroused thus: "This being is indeed glad. How good, how excellent!" . . . But if his boon companion or the dear person was happy in the past but is now unlucky and unfortunate, then *mudita* can still be aroused by remembering his past happiness and apprehending the glad aspect in this way: "In the past he had great wealth, a great following and he was always glad." Or *mudita* can be aroused by apprehending the future glad aspect in him in this way: "In the future he will again enjoy similar success and will go about in gold palanquins, on the backs of elephants or on horseback, and so on."[26]

This passage highlights a number of features of *mudita*. Most generally, it involves taking pleasure in the happiness, success, or good fortune of others. The good fortune, however, need not be taking place in the present; one can take pleasure in someone's past or future good fortune, too. Nor is it limited to another person's *spiritual* or *moral* benefits but includes mundane benefits like how comfortable and flashy their transportation is.

Though Buddhaghosa's description is in terms of the person's response, their cheerfulness or gladness, this is too wide. An addict may be very cheerful and glad upon obtaining a drug that is in fact killing him and costing him his career and family. In this case, even though the addict is glad, the situation doesn't warrant *mudita* because the event doesn't really benefit him. In the sense that the

---

26. *Visuddhimagga* IX.85–6. This translation uses the term "gladness" to translate *mudita*; I've replaced it here with the original.

addict derives *some* immediate pleasure from taking the drug, one may be able to experience *mudita* in this respect, though this would likely be outweighed by displeasure in the negative effects taking the drug will have on him and those around him.

Conspicuously absent from the description is any mention of whether or not the person *deserves* such benefits. *Mudita* involves taking pleasure in another's benefit *regardless* of whether or not they deserve to ride in a gold palanquin or a shiny new Porsche. Again if someone drives a Porsche because they exploited and killed others, the pleasure in their enjoyment of the car will *overall* be vastly outweighed by displeasure in the suffering that led to it. One can, however, be overall pleased when someone wins a Porsche in a raffle, even if the person doesn't deserve it in a variety of senses. Even if they didn't earn it, already have one, or are a painfully slow driver, one can still experience *mudita* at their good fortune.

Most importantly, experiencing *mudita* is not voluntary, though one can take voluntary action to arouse it. It is not an action, even a private mental one. One can engage in certain mental acts like thinking, visualizing, or imagining in order to cultivate the reaction, but the response *itself* is not a voluntary action. Like schadenfreude, it is commonly associated with external behaviors, but it can be present even when unexpressed. We can act as if we are pleased by another's good fortune when we really are not, and we can be pleased with another's good fortune without expressing it outwardly at all.

Mudita is thought of highly in Buddhist theory—it is described as one of the four "divine abodes" or "immeasurable states."[27] Though it is an important concept in Buddhist thought,

27. In Sanskrit, *brahmavihāra* and *apramāṇa*, respectively.

it has received little analysis about why it might count as a morally good quality.[28] Writers on *mudita* often tout the desirability of such a state, highlighting that it will increase one's pleasure and can counter the melancholia that can sometimes accompany compassion.

This may be true, but it is not enough for *mudita* to count as a moral virtue. After all, the pleasure of schadenfreude is no less pleasant to experience than that of *mudita*. A short memory might prevent compassion fatigue, but having a short memory isn't a moral virtue. Understanding the virtuousness and viciousness of pleasure via the underlying concern, however, can illuminate what makes *mudita* a moral virtue: *Mudita* is virtuous because it is a manifestation of morally important concern for the benefit and well-being of others.

To see this, it will be helpful to consider the vices to which *mudita* is opposed. *Mudita* is often contrasted with jealousy and envy, suggesting that a kind of selfishness is the root enemy of *mudita*.[29] Selfish concerns are often the main obstacles to taking pleasure in others' good fortune; it wouldn't be unusual if Peter's failure to be pleased by his colleague's career success were because *he* wanted that promotion for himself.[30]

Jealousy and envy are often the chief obstacles to *mudita*, but they are not always. Jealousy and envy paradigmatically involve

---

28. Jackson (1971, 6) lamented this lack over forty years ago. Very little has changed—as I write, a search of journals such as *Philosophy East and West* and *The Journal of Buddhist Ethics* yields mentions, but few discussions, of *mudita*.

29. *Mudita* is contrasted with envy and jealousy in recent discussions such as Sayadaw (2006) and Conze (1967/1973), and also in older texts like Buddhaghosa's *Visddhimagga* (for example, IX.95).

30. This selfish orientation is distinct from his own reactions to it: Peter may *wish* that he was pleased for his colleague but be unable to feel pleasure because he cares about his own career too much. In this case, it is virtuous that he wishes he weren't selfish, but he still is, in fact, selfish.

another person having something that we wish to have for our-selves.[31] Peter might fail to take pleasure in his colleague's promotion not because he wants it for himself but merely because he wants his colleague *not* to have it. Or perhaps Peter just doesn't care about his colleague at all one way or another and is simply bitter and displeased to hear about yet another promotion. The vices opposed to *mudita*, then, are not limited to jealousy and envy but also include malicious desires for the suffering of others and also indifference to others altogether. These vices are not rooted solely in selfishly desiring benefits, but in a more general self-centered orientation.[32]

To understand the self-centeredness that opposes *mudita*, it will be useful to think about cases of pleasure in the success of others that *do not* count as *mudita*. It is, after all, possible to take pleasure in the good fortune of others for self-centered reasons: A contractor, for example, who takes pleasure in an acquaintance being elected to public office not because he cares about his town or about democracy, but because he cares about winning city construction contracts. A mother who takes pleasure in her son's good grades not because she cares about her *son*, but because of how his grades reflect on *her* and her social standing. A husband who is pleased that his wife is happy at a new job not out of concern for *her*, but so *he* "doesn't have to sit through her whining" any longer.[33] Though these people genuinely feel pleasure at the success of another, they do not experience *mudita* because their pleasure does not manifest a concern for the other person, but rather a concern for themselves and their own situation.

---

31. See Farrell (1980, 531ff.).

32. For more on the ethics of this self-relational orientation, see Garfield (2015, 11ff.).

33. Oates discusses just this feature: "A great deal of what passes for love is really aimed at mere emotional gratification on the part of the lover, for whom the 'beloved' is little more than a prop for acting out some drama satisfying a purely subjective need—the beloved's own needs being treated less seriously" (1971, 23).

Mudita is a virtuous state because it manifests a morally good concern—a selfless concern for the well-being of other people. The various vices opposed to *mudita* are the hedonic manifestations of failing to have this concern: The jealous care too much about their own benefits, the malicious actively want others to suffer misfortunes, and the indifferent do not care about them at all.

It is important to remember that even though *mudita* is a virtuous state, not all failures to experience *mudita* count as vicious. If I fail to experience pleasure at your promotion because I do not care about what happens to you, my lack of pleasure is vicious. If I fail to be pleased because I am too exhausted, however, this does not count as vicious. The former manifests something about my orientation to others that the latter does not.

For many of us, an honest assessment of our concerns would reveal that we care too little about the well-being, goals, and successes of others. These things matter to me, but not always as much or as deeply as I would like. In general, we have an easier time feeling pleased when *we* win the game, get the applause, or land an undeserved lucky break than when others do. *Mudita* is the hedonic manifestation of the part of us that selflessly cares about others, takes their experiences seriously, and values their good fortune. Insofar as it manifests these concerns, this pleasure reflects well on one's moral character.

Of course, not everybody shares this tendency. Some people care too little about their own successes and too much for the success of others. If their *mudita* manifests this concern, it is virtuous, but they may be better off, at least for a while, avoiding such pleasure and cultivating pleasure in their own good fortune. Some of us get pleasure in our own successes for free and must work to cultivate *mudita*. Others get *mudita* for free and must work to cultivate pleasure in their own good fortunes. Though I've focused on *mudita*, the pleasure associated with both the concern for ourselves *and* for others can be virtuous in the same way. Failing to care sufficiently for oneself can also be a moral defect; it is, after all, failing to care about a human being with genuine moral worth.[34]

Though *mudita* is often expressed outwardly and intentionally cultivated, the state itself can be experienced without outward expression and, at least when things go well, comes upon us naturally as a manifestation of our deep concern for others. It makes one a better person to rejoice in the pleasures and success of others, even if unexpressed.

CONCLUSION

I have argued that pleasures and displeasures are relevant to our moral character by manifesting morally important cares or concerns. This does not, however, require that the person who experiences these pleasures or displeasures is consciously aware of such concerns. We are often unaware of our own concerns and cares—friends may see clearly that our pleasure that a hiking trip has not been cancelled stems from a romantic interest in a fellow guest rather than, as we may insist, our newfound love of the outdoors. A racist may insist that his displeasure with black neighbors is simply because he finds certain patterns of speech and music to be annoying, while we can see that it stems from a deeper racial disgust.

If Peter's displeasure at his colleague's success really manifests a concern for his colleague to suffer, it reflects poorly upon his character whether or not he is consciously aware of it. Similarly, if you feel pleased at the release of a colleague's new book but mistakenly

---

34. See Hill (1991) for more on how servility can be a moral vice.

think that it is simply because you are in a good mood when it is really because you genuinely wish the colleague well, your pleasure reflects a good character despite your lack of awareness. What is morally relevant is what concerns (or lack thereof) are manifested in pleasure or displeasure, not whether or not we consider such concerns or are aware of their connection to our pleasure and displeasure.

In discussing schadenfreude and *mudita*, I've focused on pleasure in the fortunes or misfortunes of others, but there are other similarly virtuous and vicious hedonic states. The same account can, for example, explain how *displeasure* at the misfortunes of others can be virtuous. This is the sort of sympathetic displeasure that Laura feels when she reads about the suffering of political refugees. Again, this displeasure is only virtuous if it is a manifestation of her concern for others. If her displeasure at the suffering of the refugees manifests a Nietzschean contempt for their weakness, then her displeasure is not virtuous.

As with pleasures, a lack of displeasure is not always vicious. If Laura fails to experience displeasure when reading about the plight of refugees because she doesn't care about them, then her lack of feeling is vicious. If she fails to feel displeasure because she is on a new antidepressant or exhausted after a long day at work, then her lack of displeasure is not vicious.

There can also be virtuous and vicious pleasures involving oneself rather than others. As Aristotle and his followers have emphasized, taking pleasure in one's own good qualities can itself be virtuous.[35] What explains *why* such pleasure is virtuous is that it manifests a concern for important moral goods, namely virtues themselves.[36]

35. See *NE* 1099a12 and Hursthouse (1999, 92ff.).
36. This is similar in structure to the recursive account found in Hurka (2001).

A virtuous person would, for example, be pleased to see that she has good marks on a very reliable moral report card because she cares about being a good person. She would also be pleased for, rather than jealous of, a friend who got even better marks on their report card because she cares about virtue rather than beating her friend in a moral competition. She will also be likely to feel displeasure when her own cruel thoughts or feelings of contempt arise because she cares about avoiding them.

There can also be virtuous and vicious pleasure in more conceptual or abstract things. A virtuous person will be likely to take pleasure in fair arrangements in general, feeling pleased at the state of affairs with less suffering or where everyone is respected equally. If she is inclined to abstraction, she might also take pleasure in *the ideals* of honesty or compassion themselves—not honesty as possessed by certain people or compassion directed toward particular people, but the very ideals of honesty and compassion.

Though I've argued that pleasure and displeasure can be morally virtuous or vicious, I've not claimed that the morally virtuous life must be a pleasant one overall. In many situations, being morally virtuous will involve sacrifices that make life less pleasurable overall.[37] This is especially true of those living in evil times; a virtuous person living in Rwanda in 1994 is not likely to have a pleasant life.

So, someone diagnosed with clinical depression may still be a morally virtuous person. Nor must having a pessimistic personality interfere with being a morally good person. Since things like our situation, personality, and expectations affect even morally relevant pleasures, two people may care equally about moral goods and yet experience different amounts of pleasure overall. I've not argued

37. Again, the classic description of this is in Wolf (1982).

that a moral life is more (or less) pleasant overall, only that what morally relevant pleasures and displeasures all have in common is that they manifest a concern for moral goods.

The reason that hedonic states can count as inner virtues is that they can manifest moral concern without overt action. This means that questions about how and why pleasure relates to our moral character need not center on its role in motivating such overt actions. Pleasure and displeasure themselves can be ways of manifesting cares and concerns central to being a morally good person, even when they do not result in external behavior.

Recall the Weather Watchers and those with locked-in syndrome: Even though they cannot *outwardly express* such pleasure and displeasure, they can experience schadenfreude and *mudita*. They can take pleasure in the sufferings or successes of others and in ideals like justice or honesty. They can be displeased by their own feelings of contempt or malicious thoughts that arise. As in us, these hedonic states can manifest what matters to them, what they care about, and so can make them morally better or worse.

One might object here that seeing such hedonic states as vicious in Weather Watchers or those with locked-in syndrome is simply overextending the judgment we make about agents, about those who do perform overt actions. If such states are morally relevant in agents because of their general connection with morally good or bad behaviors, then taking such pleasures and displeasures to be morally relevant in those unable to perform overt actions is simply to project such judgments where they don't belong.

I do not deny that one way in which pleasures and displeasures can be morally relevant in agents is that they tend to produce certain kinds of behaviors. I've simply argued that this is not the whole story when it comes to pleasure and moral character; some pleasure can be morally bad independently of its effect on overt action.

Even when disconnected from action, pleasure can reflect what matters to us.

Many have found the idea that pleasure can itself be morally bad to be quite compelling. A classic objection to hedonistic consequentialism, the view that morally right acts are those that maximize total pleasure, is that it "counts too much." In maximizing *all* pleasure, it mistakenly takes immoral pleasures to be relevant. It shouldn't be that rape is wrong because the rapist's pleasure is *outweighed* by the displeasure that he causes, it's that his pleasure *shouldn't count at all*.[38] It's not that the pleasure is bad *because* it leads to certain actions; it's that the pleasure is independently bad and so shouldn't count as a factor in assessing the morality of the associated action.

Similarly, I've argued that pleasure can be morally vicious not because of a connection with certain overt actions, but by manifesting a defect in moral concern. It can manifest an indifference to others or even a malicious orientation to them. Though they are often inner, private states, pleasure and displeasure can manifest an orientation to the world—to others, to the self, to arrangements, and to events. This orientation is central to moral character. It explains how pleasures can be virtuous or vicious independently of overt action. If a Weather Watcher or someone with locked-in syndrome takes pleasure in witnessing a rape or murder, it is vicious because it manifests at best an indifference to the rights and suffering of the victim, and at worse a positive relation to the violation of those rights and the creation of such suffering.

---

38. See Williams (1973/1988). Those who think that pleasure is an intrinsic good would see the rapist's pleasure as a mixed state: good as pleasure and bad as malice—see Hurka (2001, 12).

When we think of good people, we think of them as being pleased by certain things and displeased by others. Other factors may interfere, but they tend to experience *mudita* and not experience schadenfreude. Such pleasures and displeasures are part of what makes them good, even when they are unable to be expressed in external behavior. Their pleasure is a way that their moral concern manifests, even if only inwardly.

Chapter 4

Emotion

Suppose you discovered that someone you admire routinely experiences disgust and contempt for people of a certain race. Or suppose you learned that they are frequently bitter and resentful toward others who have done them no wrong. Would you think any less of them? We expect a good person to have a certain kind of emotional life: to feel gratitude toward those who benefit them, sympathy toward those who suffer, and grief when something tragic happens.

We expect a good person to have such an emotional life, not merely to project such a life outwardly. It is, of course, better if a friend doesn't express his racial contempt, but it would be best if he didn't experience it at all. We think of people we admire as not merely *expressing* gratitude, sympathy, or encouragement but as *actually feeling these things*, even if they are unable to express them. Inner emotional states are an important part of being a virtuous person.

What makes these emotional states virtuous or vicious? After a brief discussion of the nature of emotion, I will argue that emotions can be morally virtuous or vicious independently of their associated overt behaviors. They are relevant to moral character by manifesting our underlying moral cares and concerns. Though our emotions and cares are closely related, this is a contingent, psychological relationship; having cares and concerns does not necessarily entail that one will have particular emotions.

This account of virtuous and vicious emotions has two important features: First, though emotions play an important part of being a virtuous person, particular emotions are not necessary to count as a good person. That is, not all virtuous people will experience the same emotions in the same situations, and not all emotional deficits are morally vicious. Second, emotions can be morally virtuous even when they are irrational. Emotions that are unwarranted or insensitive to one's available evidence can still be morally virtuous. This best explains cases where irrational emotions still reflect well on one's moral character.

WHICH EMOTIONS?

The use of emotion as a category of our mental lives is fairly recent and by no means universal. This is evident in language: There is no single term in, for example, Tibetan or Sanskrit, that corresponds to the category. Even in English, the use of the term "emotion," formerly referring to a public disturbance, did not acquire its current meaning until the early nineteenth century (recall that early modern philosophers often preferred to write about "passions" or "sentiments" rather than the "emotions").

Even in modern English, the meaning of the terms "emotion," "feeling," "passion," and "mood" are slippery and have overlapping senses. We might sometimes call love a feeling and other times an emotion. Being cheerful or restless might be a feeling or a mood.[1]

---

1. The distinctions found in English are by no means the only way of classifying the affective realm. One can find in Indian thought, for example, a distinction between bhāva (a kind of devotional and aesthetic response), kleśas (mental clinging resulting from ignorance),

Despite this slipperiness, I will try to give a general characterization of emotions before discussing their relevance to moral character.

My discussion will center on emotions as involuntary, inner responses. Though my arguments will not rely on them, emotions are often generally taken to have other features as well. For example, they often involve bodily changes: Being angry, frightened, or aroused all involve certain bodily changes like an increased heart rate, sweating, or muscle tension.[2] They also take objects, a feature sometimes used to distinguish them from moods. I am, for example, envious *of* the success of others, proud *of* my accomplishments, amused *at* a well-timed joke, and angry *with* a rude friend.[3] They also have a duration in time; emotions arise and pass away. The range of this duration is fuzzy: When I have a bout of worry that puts me on edge for the rest of the day or week, it is difficult if not impossible to tell where the short-term emotion ends and the long-term mood begins.[4]

and *rasas* (a class of many various aesthetic responses). For more on *rasa*, see Bharata's *Nāṭyaśāstra* 31–3 (2010, 55ff.). See also Bilimoria (1995, 67ff.) for more on categories of mental states found in various strains of Indian thought.

2. Some accounts of emotion take them to be nothing more than bodily changes. This kind of account was famously defended by William James (1884) and Carl Lange (1885/1922) and a more recent version in Prinz (2004a) and (2004b). Though such theorists can accept my claims about how emotions relate to moral character, I will take emotions to have both mental and physical aspects. This is in part because there are many bodily states that do not seem to be emotions and such states are not generally relevant to moral character: Having a craving for sushi and being exhausted after a run involve bodily changes, but these are not emotions and do not say anything about one's moral character. Recall that both Descartes (*The Passions of the Soul*, I.24–5) and Hume (*Treatise* I.1.2) took passions to involve the soul in a way that bodily sensations like hunger do not.

3. Since I am not lonely, cranky, chipper, or listless *with* or *at* anything, these states are often classified as moods rather than emotions. Some states do not cleanly fall into only one of these categories: I may be bored with a philosophy talk I am attending or simply bored in general. I may be stressed over an upcoming deadline or simply stressed. Though I will focus on object-directed states, my account can allow that objectless states or states that float freely from object to object can also be virtuous or vicious.

4. For example, Oatley et al. (2006, 30) claim that emotions must have a shorter duration than moods; Annette Baier (2010, 161) suggests emotions last for "minutes rather than days."

More important for my purposes, emotions are involuntary, can be rationally assessable, and are themselves distinct from their associated behavioral expressions. Let's start with the least controversial of these characterizations: emotions as involuntary. Emotions are things that *happen to us* rather than things we *do*. Aside from existentialist philosophers, this is intuitive and widely accepted.[5] We can, of course, do things to encourage or regulate our emotions. We can mentally replay scenes in our minds, hire a therapist, or decide to take a mood-regulating drug. These actions encourage or discourage an emotional state, but the state *itself* is still involuntary.

Emotions are also distinct from their expressions in behavior. We can feel happy, afraid, or guilty without expressing it outwardly, perhaps when the costs of doing so would be very high. We can also act *as if* we feel such things when we really do not, for example, when it would be inappropriate or to spare someone's feelings.[6] This can often be morally relevant: It is important to distinguish between *being* angry (an inner state) and *behaving* angrily (an outward expression). A Buddhist who takes all anger to be harmful can still accept that *acting* angrily is often good. One might outwardly scream and shout at a teenager to stop him from using his cellphone while driving, while inwardly feeling no anger toward him. In cases like this, one acts as an angry person does but does not experience anger as an inner emotion.[7]

Nico Frijda (2007, 175ff.) claims they last from minutes to weeks and argues convincingly that duration boundary requirements are largely a matter of taste and theoretical simplicity.

5. See Adams (1985), Ekman (1992a and 1992b), Ben-Ze'ev (2000), and Roberts (2003) among many others. Sartre (1948/1993) and Solomon (1998) endorse the minority view that emotions are voluntary actions.

6. Baier's "Getting in Touch with Our Own Feelings" (2010, 123ff.) highlights the common gulf between what our emotions are and what we express.

7. These are instances of what is known in Sanskrit as *upāya* or "skillful means." Epictetus suggests a similar position about trivial grief: Though he takes grief over material loss to be

Emotions are also rationally assessable. Some emotions are warranted, and others are not. The fear of being attacked by a drunken bar patron who has threatened you is warranted in a way that the fear of being attacked by an oak tree is not. The former is *rational*, while the latter is not. What allows for this is that emotions have a connection to the world; they, in part, represent the world as being a certain way. Though different theories of emotion describe the exact nature of this aspect in very different ways, emotions involve taking the world to be a certain way.[8] This is present in the analysis of many particular emotions: So fear involves representing danger and gratitude involves representing a benefit. This allows them to be rational or irrational; they can make sense given the way the world is, or at least our view of it.

Being rational or warranted in this sense is different from being useful or appropriate. If a very good student is anxious over an upcoming exam, her anxiety may be unwarranted as she is in no danger of failing it. Her worries are *unjustified*; given her abilities, it is unreasonable for her to feel anxious. This anxiety may, however, still be *useful* or *beneficial*—it may cause her to prepare more, get a good night's sleep, and pay close attention in class.[9]

Being warranted is also different from being appropriate: If Tom learns that a close friend has betrayed him while in church or at a

---

vicious, he also notes that expressing such grief outwardly can often be a good thing, as when comforting a friend who is upset—see *Enchiridion* 16.

8. The Stoics took emotions to involve judgments about the world; see DeBrabander (2004, 202–203) and Long (2002, 213ff.). More recently, Robert Solomon (2007) has defended this view. Others describe emotions as involving beliefs; see Kenny (1963), Marks (1982), and Ben-Ze'ev (2000, 52ff.). Roberts (1988) describes them as involving construals, while Charland (1997) takes them to be representations. Hursthouse simply talks of emotions as having "ideas" or "thoughts" (1999, 111) about the world. I will not presume a particular theory of how emotions are connected with the world in my discussion.

9. I owe this distinction to a helpful discussion with Nomy Arpaly.

meditation retreat, his anger may be warranted (Tom *was* in fact wronged by his friend) but not appropriate (feeling anger is not fitting, given the situation). Similarly, feeling fear when watching a horror film does not seem to be *inappropriate*; a horror film is an acceptable situation in which to feel afraid. But such fear may still be *unwarranted* because the representations about danger it includes are unwarranted.[10] We say to children who have been frightened by a movie, not that their fear is inappropriate, but that it is "just a movie" and is "nothing to be scared of"—that it is unwarranted.[11]

Finally, at least some emotions do not necessarily involve behavioral action. Of course, in everyday life, emotions often are associated with certain overt actions. These associated actions are not, however, necessary conditions for the emotion in the same way that representations and concerns are: A student cannot be joyful about having passed an exam unless she takes herself to have passed it and cares about passing it. She can, however, feel such joy without being able to outwardly act on or express it. Someone with locked-in syndrome can feel a rush of emotions when their estranged son comes to visit them, even though they will be unable to express such emotions outwardly.

Some theorists have thought that the very concept of an emotion entails a tendency to overt action, or at least the search for an action.[12] This does not, however, seem to be required by the

---

10. I assume here, contra Walton (1990), that we do feel genuine fear toward what we take to be fictions. This is not, however, essential to my claims.

11. D'Arms and Jacobson (2000) defend this distinction at length.

12. This view can be found clearly in the work of Frijda, who straightforwardly claims, "Emotions are action tendencies" (1987, 71). He is followed in this by Jon Elster, who claims these tendencies are not merely dispositions, but "already triggered by the emotion" (2004, 151n4). Jesse Prinz endorses the weaker claim that emotions must "instigate the search for appropriate actions" (2004b, 228). I am not alone in denying this—see also Roberts (2003, 63).

concept: It is easy to imagine the sentient Weather Watchers made out of stone feeling disappointment, anger, or joy when the weather changes. Such creatures could experience the mental and somatic aspects of emotion just as we do: As living beings, they can have a circulatory system and experience an increased or decreased heart rate. As creatures with a mental life, they can represent the world in the same way we do, as dangerous, wonderful, or terrible. This is compatible with an inability to perform overt actions. Imagining the emotions of these creatures does not involve some conceptual contradiction, even though they have no capacity for overt action at all.

More realistically, someone who has locked-in syndrome after a stroke loses their ability to perform overt actions but does not thereby lose their emotional life. Feelings of frustration, loneliness, and isolation are common, even though these are not expressed outwardly. Even without the capacity to act, people experience a variety of emotions as inner states. This is a large part of what is heartbreaking about locked-in syndrome; one's emotional life is left unchanged as one's connection with the external, social world is largely severed.

Even able-bodied people may feel emotions without acting, planning to act, or searching for action. Consider a father who feels so disappointed in his son that he has given up not only any action regarding his son but thinking about him altogether. Part of the character of some negative emotions like depression or despair is that they often *remove* the will to act or even search for action—that is partly what makes them so damn difficult to overcome.[13] Even

---

13. A more obscure example of this might be the Greek *acedia*, a kind of listlessness usually applied to monks and nuns characterized by an inability to work or pray—see Taylor (2006, 19).

positive emotions can have this feature: If a student currently feels satisfaction about her answers on last week's exam, what action is she searching for?

VIRTUOUS AND VICIOUS EMOTIONS

Emotions can be morally virtuous or vicious. This is distinct from the role they might play in living a flourishing, meaningful, or psychologically healthy human life. It is also distinct from (and compatible with) other ways in which emotions are morally important. Emotions may also be relevant to making moral judgments, having morally praiseworthy motives, moral development, and leading a flourishing life more generally. These are difficult and interesting questions, but here I am concerned with how emotions can, independently of associated behaviors, make one a morally better or worse person.[14]

This question is importantly different from questions of whether or not we can be praised or blamed for our emotions. It has seemed clear to many that emotions cannot be virtuous or vicious because they are involuntary; since we cannot be held responsible for involuntary states, they can't say anything about our moral character.[15]

---

14. Many, such as Hursthouse (1999, 108), find a friend in Aristotle here, citing his claim that virtues are concerned with actions *and* feelings (*NE* 1104b14). The fact that emotions and actions are often treated together makes Aristotle difficult to interpret on this topic; Kosman (1980, 109), for example, suggests that only complexes of emotions *and* actions count as virtues for Aristotle.

15. Aristotle says that emotions themselves cannot count as virtues because virtues are related to *choice* (*NE* 1139a22–3). Aquinas follows him in this: "If then the passions be considered in themselves, to wit, as movements of the irrational appetite, thus there is no moral good or evil in them" (*Summa* II Q.24).

Even if we cannot be blameworthy for involuntary states, such states can still make one a morally worse person.[16] Even if someone with involuntary racist emotions is not *blameworthy* for those emotions, they still reflect poorly on his moral character. He would, after all, be a *better* person if he did not have those emotions. Learning that someone feels racial contempt, greed, or envy leads us to revise our assessment of their moral character even if we know that they can't help but have such feelings. We wish, for example, for our children to grow up free from these emotions because we want them to be the better people.

Blame and viciousness are distinct moral evaluations. If nature has made it so that I cannot help but have sexist attitudes, nature has thereby made me vicious. If I truly have no control over my attitudes, I may not be responsible for such attitudes. But that is a separate question; in any case, such attitudes are a blemish on my moral character, and I would be a better person without them.

It is important to distinguish an emotion from one's response to it. Two people might both have feelings of racial disgust, but one reacts to them with pride while the other is ashamed or disgusted. Both may have a first-order vicious emotion, while their second-order emotional responses are very different. The disgust or shame of the latter is virtuous because it manifests a concern not to have such emotions.[17]

---

16. Some philosophers have defended this view of blame. According to Hume, "*sentiments* are every day experienced of blame and praise, which have objects beyond the dominion of the will or choice" (*Enquiry* IV.268, 322). More recently, Adams (1985) argues that we can be blameworthy for involuntary states of mind.

17. This is similar to the Buddhist concept known in Pāli as *hiri*, which is often translated as "shame." It is a kind of moral embarrassment that the Indian philosopher Buddhaghosa characterizes as anxiety or disgust at evil (*Visuddhimagga* XIV.142). In this sense, it is similar to Aristotle's discussion of *aidōs* (also often translated as "shame" or "modesty"), though he denies that this feeling can be virtuous (see *NE* 1128b10ff.). For a detailed discussion of *hiri*, see Heim (2012).

In its most simple form, my answer to the question of when emotions are virtuous or vicious is this: Emotions are virtuous or vicious when they manifest morally important cares or concerns (or a lack of such concerns). This type of care or concern is not itself an emotion. It is, for example, not episodic in the same way as emotions. Richard cares about the Red Sox even when he is reading a book about philosophy or sleeping. Tenzin cares about his mother even when he is not currently feeling warm feelings toward her, when distracted with his work or watching a movie.

Let's start with the idea that emotions can, and often do, manifest our underlying cares and concerns. This is evident in everyday life. When my roommate is annoyed at our neighbor's loud music, it manifests her concern for peace and quiet. When a high school English teacher gets annoyed at my split infinitives, he manifests his concern for certain prescriptive grammar rules. A graduate student's joy at the warm reception her advisor gives her paper manifests that she cares about writing good papers and about the opinion of her advisor. As Annette Baier puts it, our emotions "will speak the truth about if and how much something matters to us."[18]

It is also important to keep in mind that the object of the emotion and the object of the concern that the emotion manifests need not be the same. When my balance is too low because of an error on the part of the bank, I am angry at *the bank*, but my anger manifests concern with *my money*.

Having the same emotion toward the same object does not always manifest the same concern. Consider different people who all feel disappointment over a baseball player strike. For some fans, it might manifest concerns over the decline of Americana, a concern for baseball as a venerable cultural institution. For others,

18. Baier (2010, 166).

it might only manifest a concern for the prospects of their favorite team. For a sports columnist, it might manifest a concern for a steady paycheck. A non–sports fan might also feel disappointment at the strike because baseball cheers up so many people he knows, manifesting a concern for the happiness of his friends. All of these people feel the same emotion toward the same event, but the emotion manifests vastly different concerns in each person.[19]

In many cases, an emotion's underlying concern is moral. When the concerns that an emotion manifests are morally important, they reflect well on one's moral character. Consider two people who feel joy at the release of hostages. For one it manifests a concern for the well-being of those in danger, but for another, it manifests a concern for filling airtime on a twenty-four-hour news network. The joy of the former is virtuous in a way that the latter is not, even though both experience the same emotion at the same event. The virtuous joy reflects well on the person's moral character because it is an emotional manifestation of concern for others. The concern to fill airtime on TV news is not morally good, so the emotional manifestation of this concern does not reflect well on the person's moral character.

This emotional reaction can be virtuous even if it goes unexpressed in one's overt behavior. It can manifest morally important concern even if the hostages were released in a faraway country and there is no action to be taken. Someone in a politically repressive situation can feel this emotion, even though expressing it may be far too dangerous for those around them. Even without any behavioral

---

19. One might think that since they feel these emotions toward the object under different descriptions that they are all actually feeling different emotions. They do at least feel emotions with the same valence toward the same object. What is important for my purposes is that the underlying concern is what determines what the emotion says about the person's character.

manifestation, the affective response of relief can manifest concern for others and so reflect well on one's moral character.[20]

The same goes for vicious emotions. These emotions manifest either a lack of moral concern or malevolent concerns. When an onlooker is angry that another person was not killed in a natural disaster or happily relieved when someone *is* killed, their emotions reflect poorly on their moral character. This is because they manifest at best an indifference to the well-being of another person, and at worst a positive concern to harm another. These emotions manifest at least a lack of concern for an important moral good, and perhaps also that they care about something morally bad (the death of another person), and so reflect poorly on their moral character. These emotional responses manifest such concerns even when unexpressed in overt behavior—someone can silently experience them without any outward expression.

It can seem, however, that *some* emotions are inherently virtuous or vicious. After all, aren't compassion and sympathy *themselves* virtuous? Aren't malice and contempt intrinsically vicious? This may be so, but when we take certain emotions to be categorically virtuous or vicious, we build moral concern into their definition.

An easy way to see this is to consider seemingly vicious instances of virtuous emotions and vice versa. Consider sympathy: If we take sympathy to be merely sharing a feeling with someone, there can be cases of vicious sympathy. Think of sharing in the feelings of those whose emotions are self-destructive: an anorexic person who feels overweight and wants to skip yet another meal or a depressed scholar who feels a strong desire to sabotage her own work. Simply sharing in the feelings and desires of these people is not always virtuous.

---

20. Emotions like these are relevant to what I have called private solidarity; for a more detailed discussion see Bommarito (2016).

One could share in these feelings *because* one wants things to get worse for them. A malicious acquaintance could sympathize with them because they want the anorexic person's health to deteriorate or the scholar to give up on her work. As the French philosopher André Comte-Sponville put it: "Sympathy in horror is a horrible sympathy."[21]

Someone who takes sympathy to be categorically virtuous is likely to reply that such cases are not instances of *real* sympathy. What, then, must be added to simply sharing a feeling with someone to get *real* sympathy? What is missing is concern for the person's well-being. For someone who takes sympathy to be categorically virtuous, true sympathy requires a concern for the well-being of the object of sympathy.[22] It is only by building in this concern that the emotion is virtuous. The point here is not that either definition of the term "sympathy" is the correct one, only that *if* sympathy is to count as categorically virtuous, then it must build morally important cares or concerns into its definition.

The same can be said for emotions that are sometimes thought to be categorically vicious; built into the very notion of these emotions is either morally bad concern or moral indifference. If malice, for example, is an emotion, then it is categorically vicious by building a concern for harming others into the very idea.

In the case of envy, for example, a selfish concern and indifference to others is often built into the emotion. Insofar as envy is categorically vicious, part of what it means to envy is to wish for

21. Comte-Sponville (1996/2001, 105).
22. Even this is not quite enough: A gambler's sympathy with an injured football player might manifest a concern for the player's well-being, but only because he has wagered a large sum of money on an upcoming game. The gambler is concerned for the well-being of the player, but only as a means to getting money. The moral concern that is required is *noninstrumental* concern for the well-being of the person we sympathize with.

yourself something that someone else has.[23] When envy is most vicious, it involves concern for others to have less of what we want. This can explain why some cases of envy are *less* vicious than others. It is less vicious (or, if you'd prefer, more virtuous) for me to envy the Dalai Lama's compassion than for me to envy my friend's good looks because the former at least manifests a concern for a moral good, compassion.

This envy is not completely virtuous, however, because it also manifests self-centered concern: *I* want to have the Dalai Lama's compassion for *myself*, and I might even want the Dalai Lama to have *less* of it—particularly if what I want is to be *more* compassionate than him (and perhaps everyone else). These concerns, even though they involve a morally valuable quality, still involve a selfishness that makes them vicious. Simply wanting to be morally better is not vicious, but it is vicious, in a subtle way, to want to be *more* moral than others (especially if this involves wanting them to be *less* moral!).

Again, this virtuous sympathy or vicious envy does not require any overt action. I can be envious of my friend's new sports car or jealous of a colleague's professional fame without ever expressing such feelings in action. It is possible for a Weather Watcher to being envious of another Weather Watcher's more pleasant location, even though it lacks overt behavior altogether. Someone with locked-in syndrome can still envy the good fortune of others or sympathize with the hardships of others, even though they are unable to act on such emotions. Insofar as such emotions manifest their cares and concerns, they make a difference to moral character. Other things equal, an envious Weather Watcher is morally worse than one who lacks such emotions; someone with locked-in syndrome

---

23. See Farrell (1980, 531) for more on this.

who sympathizes with others is more admirable than someone who does not.

Again, none of this is to say that envy is categorically vicious or sympathy is categorically virtuous. It is simply to say that someone who *does* think of them that way will have moral concerns built into the notion. For them, what distinguishes vicious faux sympathy or virtuous faux envy from *real* sympathy and envy will be the moral concerns underlying them.

Most emotions, however, do not have such moral considerations built into them and resist categorizations as *always* virtuous or *always* vicious. Growing up Catholic and American, one will run into very different uses of the term "pride"—at school one is told that it is good to take pride in your work, while at church one is told that pride is one of the deadly sins. Neither use of the term "pride" is incorrect, but this difference can be understood in terms of what concerns each version manifests. If someone's pride in a well-written essay manifests a deep concern for good writing, it is not vicious. When a father's pride in his child's successes manifests his care for the child, it reflects well on him. It is in this sense that "taking pride in yourself" can be virtuous; it can manifest morally relevant self-respect.

When pride is vicious, it manifests excessive concern for oneself or for trivial things. This can be a matter of emphasis: Whereas pride in my *well-written* essay manifests a nonvicious concern for quality, pride in *my* well-written essay can manifest a more self-centered concern. If my pride is vicious, it is because it manifests not a concern to do well, but simply to do better than another person.[24] Vicious pride is pride that stems from a concern to puff up one's own ego, a lack of

---

24. This comes through in Spinoza's description of vainglory: "he who at last comes off conqueror boasts more because he has injured another person than because he profited himself. This glory of self-satisfaction, therefore is indeed vain, for it is really no glory" (*Ethics* IV, prop. 58). This will be relevant to my later discussion of modesty.

concern for others, and the malicious desire to injure others. Such concerns manifest morally bad concerns and so are vicious.

EMOTION AND CONCERN

So far, I've argued that emotions are virtuous or vicious by manifesting morally relevant cares and concerns. The relationship between emotions and the concerns they manifest is complicated and worth discussing in detail. I'll focus on two important features of this relationship: First, the intensity of an emotion is often not proportionate to the degree of concern; stronger emotions do not always mean stronger concern. Second, caring about something does not necessarily entail having certain emotions. When we care about something, we will *in general* experience certain emotions, but this is a contingent psychological fact. These features will be relevant for understanding when emotional deficits count as morally vicious and when they do not and for explaining variation in the emotional lives of virtuous people.

In real life, our emotions manifest many different concerns at once, often a mix of moral and nonmoral concerns. My relief upon hearing that a colleague has returned safely from a long trip manifests *both* my concern for her well-being *and* my concern to hear the comments she has on my paper. If someone cuts in front of me while I am in line at the grocery store, my anger will likely manifest concerns for fairness, not to be publicly insulted, and to get home quickly. This is not a problem for my account; my relief over my colleague's safe return or my anger over being cut in line is morally virtuous only *to the degree* that it manifests moral concerns.[25]

---

25. See Bommarito (2017) for a more detailed treatment of how this account applies to anger and righteous indignation.

More intense emotions do not always mean deeper or more intense concern. Of two students who are angry over failing an exam, it does not necessarily follow that the angrier student cares more about doing well in the class. Perhaps the angrier one simply had unrealistic expectations about how well they would do; the other student, having always been realistic about their dismal chances of passing, was able to take the failure in stride because they saw it coming more clearly. Or perhaps the angrier student feels more intense emotions because they are in the early stages of giving up smoking, or because their parents are going through a hostile divorce. Many factors other than one's degree of concern affect emotional intensity.

It can be tempting to think of the virtuous person's emotions as being proportionate to the goodness or badness of their objects.[26] And yet a wide variety factors aside from one's degree of concern can affect the intensity of one's emotions, many of which do not reflect on one's moral character. What is important is that the virtuous person's concern is proportionate to the importance of its object; a virtuous person will *care* more about more important things. A variety of situational and psychological factors having nothing to do with one's moral character can affect the intensity of the emotional manifestation of this concern. It is not a defect of moral character to have a calm temperament or to have a stressful career, though these factors will alter the intensity of one's emotions in various ways.

This allows for variations in culture and individual temperament. Even if it is true that people from southern Italy feel more intense anger, say, when a friend makes a bad decision than people from Finland, it does not follow that Italians *care* more about their friends. It simply means that their care is more likely to manifest

---

26. See Hurka (2001, 83ff.).

in a particular way.[27] Again, consider two students who have both failed the first exam in a class. Though both care deeply about doing well, in one this care manifests as sadness and in the other as anger. Neither emotion is the "correct" one; each is a way in which a concern about the course is manifested emotionally.

It might seem that though neither anger nor sadness is the uniquely correct manifestation of concern for doing well in the class, perhaps emotions like joy would be incorrect. Even joy at a failed exam, however, *can* manifest a concern to do well in the class. Consider Dana, a deeply optimistic student. She does not have to *try* to be optimistic to console herself, but has an unflagging positivity "in her bones." One imagines Dana explaining to her friend that she is happy to have failed the exam because it's good to make mistakes early in the course so now she knows how to better direct her studying. Also, she's heard from others that it's much better to have an upward trajectory in grades so it's better to fail an exam early in the semester, and so on. Here Dana's concern to do well in the class is refracted through her optimism and comes out as joy. It is not particular emotions that reflect well on someone as a student, but rather the concerns that such emotions manifest.

It would be useful for my account if care or concern conceptually entailed having certain emotions. It can be tempting to think that someone who cares about something will, simply in virtue of what it means to care, feel fear when it is threatened, angry when it is slighted, and happy when it flourishes. If this were true, certain emotions would count as virtuous because they are part of what it means to care about something. This would be beneficial for my argument

27. That is, if there is a difference between the intensity of the emotion and not merely its outward expression. Beyond appeals to cultural stereotypes and "national character," there is evidence that emotional responses do vary between cultures; see Tsai, Levenson, and McCoy (2006). Wolf (2011) takes on similar themes with regard to blame.

because particular emotional states would then be conceptually entailed by moral concern. I do not, however, think this is true.

Though our emotions and cares *are* deeply related, care does not entail particular emotions. Rather, the close relationship between concern and particular emotions is a contingent, psychological fact. It is possible, both conceptually and psychologically, to care about things despite lacking particular emotions. Having an emotion may well require that one cares about *something*; someone who doesn't care about *anything at all* may be incapable of experiencing any emotion at all. If nothing matters to me at all, I cannot feel frustration, joy, or fear.[28]

But even if emotion requires care, not all care requires emotion. A student who cares about doing well in class can, coldly and without emotion, form a strong resolve to improve after failing an exam. A surgeon might even purposely take steps to extinguish her emotions regarding her work *because* she cares deeply about her patients and doing so helps her to perform better in the operating room. To the extent that she succeeds in this aim, she will continue to care about her patients' lives, but this concern will not manifest as emotion. In fact, her lack of emotion, if cultivated out of genuine concern for her patients, reflects well on her moral character.

If it makes sense in particular cases to have cares and concerns without an emotional manifestation, then it is at least conceptually possible in all cases. If a student can care about doing well in class despite lacking any emotions *today*, then couldn't she do so for the entire semester? Or for her entire life? It may be psychologically

---

28. There may be some exceptions to this, depending on how permissive your definition of emotion is. If surprise, detached amusement, and depression count as emotions, then perhaps such a person could experience some version of a limited range of emotions that includes these. These are, however, not clear cases of emotion and my focus will be on cases of genuine care or concern in the absence of particular emotions.

implausible, but need not be conceptually self-contradictory, to imagine a being who cares about many things but whose cares never manifest as emotion. Such a being is like the concerned but emotionless surgeon, but about everything.

If this sounds far-fetched, consider the kinds of ideal agents sometimes posited by Kantian moral philosophers. Such agents are motivated only by respect for The Moral Law and not by inclinations. The term "inclinations" is, of course, a catchall that includes not only emotions but also most desires, pleasures, and preferences—anything that is not concern for one's moral duty. This character is usually deployed in debates about what the morally praiseworthy motives for action are, but insofar as respect for moral duty is not an emotion, it also paints a picture of emotionless moral concern. Such an ideal agent cares deeply about The Moral Law, but without any emotional responses.[29] I am not endorsing the idea that this is psychologically possible for normal human beings, nor am I endorsing it as a morally ideal way to live. I'm merely pointing out that many philosophers have taken such a character to be a *conceptually coherent* ideal; the description itself does not involve a contradiction.

There is also more empirical support for the idea that concern does not require particular emotions. Consider the case of a man, known as N.M., who, after damaging part of his brain, became unable to experience emotions like fear and anger.[30] After his brain was damaged, he described himself as adopting an "Eastern philosophy" approach to life and said he rarely, if ever, experienced fear

---

29. Whether or not Kantian respect is an emotion is, like so much of Kant interpretation, disputed. I mean here to be referring to what McCarty (1993) calls the "intellectualist view," which sees respect for the moral law as involving "purely intellectual recognition" (423). McCarty characterizes this as the reigning view, attributing it to Robert Paul Wolff and Onora O'Neill among others.
30. Specifically, "bilateral amygdala damage and a left thalamic lesion" (Sprengelmeyer et al. 1999, 2451).

or anger even in difficult or frustrating situations. According to the study, N.M. came to enjoy activities like

> hunting Jaguars at the upper course of the Orinoco river, or hunting deer in Siberia while hanging on a rope under a helicopter. In these kinds of situations, he said that he always experienced excitement but never fear.[31]

His self-reports were also confirmed by his inability to recognize facial expressions of fear and anger.

Despite being unable to experience anger or fear, N.M. was still able to care about many things, even those normally associated with fear and anger. Continuing to work for a German company as a salesman, one assumes that he continued to care about doing his job well. One presumes that it still mattered to him whether or not a client decided to buy his product, even though he no longer felt fear when in danger of losing an account or anger during difficult meetings. And even when hunting Jaguars or dangling from a helicopter, he continued to care about whether he lived or died. After all, though he did dangerous things, he didn't do *stupid* things—excitement is one thing; *recklesness* is another. He did more dangerous things than many, but he did not do totally reckless things like trying to walk the Sahara without water or jumping off a tall building without a parachute.

N.M. seems to be someone who *cares* about his own safety and his business interests despite the fact that such concerns do not manifest as fear or anger.[32] Cases like this show that it is possible, though perhaps rare, to care about things while failing to experience

---

31. Sprengelmeyer et al. (1999, 2455). The details described earlier are from the same source.
32. Tim Schroeder makes a similar observation when discussing the same case: "N.M appears to care about whether he lives or dies, to care about whether or not he is cheated in business dealings, and so on, but his emotions do not respond as though he does care" (2004, 34).

particular emotions. This is not to say that the two are not related in deep and important ways; in human psychology in general, emotions and concerns *are* importantly connected. If we meet someone who *never* feels *any* emotions about a cause or person, it is still a good bet that they don't care very much about it. It is not, however, a conceptual certainty.

EMOTIONAL FAILURE:
TWO COLD CHARACTERS

Our cares and concerns manifest in our emotional lives not only as emotions we *do* have but also as emotions we *fail* to have. But not all of these emotional failures are relevant to our moral character. If N.M. fails to get indignant over political corruption, it is not vicious because his lack of indignation does not manifest a lack of concern. His lack of emotion does not count against his moral character; he is unlike someone who fails to get angry because they don't care about justice. This means that failing to feel the right emotion, at the right time, toward the right object is not always morally vicious.

Many philosophers have taken certain emotions, or emotional capacities, to be essential for being a virtuous person. The Chinese philosopher Mengzi praises the "Four Sprouts," which include a capacity for feelings like pity, compassion, and shame. Without these sprouts, he claims, one would be vicious and fail to be fully human.[33] Similarly, David Hume talks about certain natural passions being central to moral virtue.[34] Those in Aristotelian tradition

---

33. *Mengzi* 2A6.
34. See especially *Treatise* III.3. Of course, the mere fact that something is natural for humans or essential to being human is not enough to make it a virtue. It is, after all, also human

see certain emotions as an essential part of our natural and distinctly human function. For them, the virtuous person will feel the right emotion, toward the right object, at the right time and in the right way—any failure to do so is vicious.[35]

And yet not all emotional failures are morally vicious, and not all emotional incapacities make one a morally worse person. A lack of feeling can, and often does, manifest a lack of concern: My roommate's lack of annoyance at our loud neighbors manifests his lack of concern for peace and quiet. My lack of feeling about how the World Series turned out manifests my lack of concern for baseball. Not all emotional failures, however, manifest a lack of concern. A devout baseball fan might fail to have any feelings about the World Series not because he doesn't care, but because he is exhausted from a long week at work or because he has a bad case of the flu.

It's not only short periods of illness or exhaustion than can affect one's emotional responses. One can fail to have particular emotions because, like N.M., they have damage to their brains. Other factors irrelevant to moral character can interfere with one's emotional capacities. For instance, various medications have been known to alter or limit people's emotional capacities.[36] Someone who starts hypertension medication or painkillers does not necessarily become a morally worse person, even when such things can diminish their

nature to be selfish and prejudiced against outsiders, but this does not make the emotions associated with greed or sexism virtuous. If human nature has made me sexist and greedy, then human nature has made me *vicious*. This can be seen clearly when it comes to epistemic virtue and vice: Even though it is human nature to succumb to the gambler's fallacy, this does not make me a better epistemic agent to do so.

35. See Hursthouse (1999) for the canonical modern statement of this view.

36. Various antidepressants and antipsychotics, of course, can affect a person's emotional responses. Medications not aimed at treating psychological symptoms can also have this effect. For example, beta-blockers such as propranol, often used to treat hypertension, can result in reduced anxiety—see Elman et al. (1998). There is also evidence that more mundane medications like acetaminophen, commonly known as Tylenol, can blunt one's emotional responses—see Durso et al. (2015). Thanks to Christopher Yamamoto for help with these references.

emotional responses. Though their emotional range and intensity may be reduced, this does not necessarily mean that they care about things less than they did before.

Differences in emotional intensity can result from temperamental differences from person to person. Jealousy, for example, can often manifest concern for a relationship. Someone might fail to be jealous of their partner's attention to another person because they don't *care* about the relationship. Another person, however, might fail to be jealous simply because they "aren't the jealous type." If one's partner fails to be jealous because they *don't care*, the failure counts against them as a partner (it would, for example, count as a reason to end the relationship). If they are simply not the jealous type, however, their lack of feeling does not count against them as a partner—given their temperament, a lack of jealousy does not mean they don't deeply value the relationship.[37]

The same is true in moral cases; not *every* failure to have an emotion reflects poorly on one's character. Not every failure to be relieved that that a friend is safe after a dangerous trip or failure to be upset when learning of an injustice reflects poorly on one's moral character. To count as vicious, lacking an emotion must manifest a *lack* of morally relevant concern (or perhaps a positively bad moral concern). If I fail to be relieved upon learning that my mother is safe after a dangerous journey because I am sleep deprived or heavily medicated, my lack of feeling does not manifest a lack of concern. As long as it does not affect my concern for my mother's well-being, the medication did not make me morally vicious. If the medication doesn't alter what matters to me, but merely limits its emotional manifestation, one need not list "moral vice" among the side effects on the medication's label. If I am not relieved because I *don't care* about my mother's safety, however, my lack of feeling manifests a defect of character, a morally relevant lack of concern. A coworker's lack of indignation over discrimination in our workplace is vicious if it manifests a lack of concern for fairness, but not if it is because they simply have a calm temperament.

Again, this is true even when the relief is not or cannot be expressed. The relief may be about an event in the past about which there is nothing to be done. I might simply think to myself, "I'm glad the plane landed safely—What a scare!" while appearing, from the outside, exactly as the calm person next to me. Emotions and emotional failures can manifest a lack of concern even when they are unexpressed and do not produce any behaviors (or failures to behave). After all, even Weather Watchers or those who are paralyzed can feel or fail to feel relief for a similarly wide variety of reasons.

Failures to have certain affective states like emotions are not categorically virtuous or vicious. Such failures are only relevant to moral character when they manifest moral concern or a lack thereof. This difference can be seen clearly in the moral difference between those with psychopathy and those with autism. Both disorders are, among other things, characterized by emotional deficits—a lack of certain emotional responses, particularly social emotions like guilt, regret, shame, and empathy. Though both conditions involve similar emotional impairments, psychopaths are morally vicious while those with autism are not.

First let's consider psychopathy. On most understandings, psychopathy involves emotional impairment. An inability to feel a wide range of emotions, specifically other-regarding emotions like empathy, guilt, and remorse, is central.[38] Jon Ronson

---

38. This is prominent in many discussions of psychopathy; see Blair et al. (2005), Herpertz and Sass (2000), and Hare (1993).

describes an interaction with a mass murderer from Haiti who confided the following: "I don't feel empathy . . . It's not a feeling I have. It's not an emotion I have. Feeling sorry for people? . . . I don't feel sorry for people. No."[39] Though psychopaths often mimic these emotions and use emotional terminology, they lack any first-personal experience of these emotions. They know the words, but not the music. Robert Hare offers the example of a psychopath who claimed that he felt remorse about a murder he committed, only to later admit that he did not "feel bad inside" about it.[40]

In addition to emotional impairment, psychopathy is also strongly associated with what is over-clinically termed "antisocial behavior"—not only criminal behavior like bullying, stealing, and assault, but also using people purely for selfish ends like sex, money, or status. In the case of criminal offenses, convicted psychopaths are three times more likely to reoffend than nonpsychopaths.[41] Of course, not all criminals or self-centered people are psychopaths. That these behaviors are associated with psychopathy is important as *evidence* that psychopaths don't simply fail to have social emotions but fail to care about others at all; at the heart of psychopathy is a lack of *concern* for the well-being and rights of others. Consider the following testimony from a psychopath convicted of kidnapping, rape, and extortion:

> Do I care about other people? That's a tough one. But yeah, I guess I really do . . . but I don't let my feelings get in the way . . . I mean, I'm as warm and caring as the next guy, but let's face it, everyone's trying to screw you . . . Do I feel bad if I have

39. Ronson (2011, 134).
40. Hare (1993, 41).
41. Blair et al. (2005, 16).

hurt someone? Yeah, sometimes. But mostly it's like . . . uh . . . [laughs] . . . how did you feel the last time you squashed a bug?[42]

The lack of certain emotions is strongly associated with the characterization that "Psychopaths view people as little more than objects to be used for their own gratification."[43] Psychopaths don't experience social emotions because they don't *care* about other people— the life of another person matters to them as much as the life of a bug. The emotional deficit in psychopaths manifests an underlying lack of concern for other people.[44]

Contrast this with cases of autism.[45] Like psychopathy, autism is also characterized by, among other things, an emotional impairment—particularly of more complex, social emotions.[46] The *Diagnostic and Statistical Manual of Mental Disorders* includes "lack of social or emotional reciprocity" as a symptom of autism.[47] Autism is, of course, not associated with criminal behavior. But the associated emotional impairment can, at least on the surface, seem a lot like that of psychopaths. Consider Temple Grandin, an autistic person described by Oliver Sacks in his book *An Anthropologist on Mars*. She describes her reaction to a college roommate who was

---

42. Quoted in Hare (1993, 33).
43. Hare (1993, 44).
44. This is a theme of many of the essays found in Schramme (2014).
45. The term "autism" is an umbrella term that covers a wide range of factors aside from the emotional element I will focus on (including, for example, repetitive behaviors and verbal communication impairment). I will focus on cases of what is called "high-functioning autism" including Asperger's syndrome. Though those with "low-functioning autism" can pose special challenges for moral theory in general, much of what I say will also apply to them.
46. The exact nature of the emotional deficits associated with autism is complex, though there is evidence that those with autism experience and understand basic emotions like anger, sadness, and happiness. They, however, have emotional deficiencies regarding more complex, social emotions like envy, pride, embarrassment, and guilt—see Capps et al. (1992), Losh and Capps (2006), and Shamay-Tsoory (2008).
47. *DSM-IV*, 299.80.

infatuated with her science teacher: "She was overwhelmed with emotion. I thought, he's nice, I can see why she likes him. But there was no more than that." Her own explanation for this lack of understanding was simply: "The emotion circuit's not hooked up—that's what's wrong."[48]

Stephanie Mayberry, diagnosed with Asperger's syndrome, describes herself as similarly baffled by emotion:

> A lady at work tried to teach me how to "read" facial expressions. She went into this long explanation, telling me that I should pay attention to what emotions I am feeling and what I think that person is feeling or may feel at that time. I was polite. I listened and said "okay" a bunch of times. But it made no sense. I am not an emotional person and I don't understand emotions in other people.[49]

The first-person accounts of autism often feature comparisons with robots and aliens—Mayberry's account is entitled "Alien: A Story of Asperger's Syndrome" and Temple Grandin describes her favorite character from the TV show *Star Trek*, an emotionless robot named Data. According to Sacks, "A surprising number of people with autism identify with Data, or with his predecessor, Mr. Spock."[50]

Under the influence of certain theories, all this talk about aliens and robots can make those with autism seem, at least in the emotional realm, pretty vicious. After all, don't they lack the "fellow feeling" so important to Hume or at least a few of the "Four Sprouts" that are essential to humanity for Mengzi? In lacking these emotional responses they lack part of the human functioning important

48. Sacks (1995, 286).
49. Mayberry (2012, 433).
50. Sacks (1995, 275).

to Aristotle and his followers. For many thinkers, they will count as vicious because they lack many of the *right* emotions.

And yet an autistic person is not a morally worse person simply in virtue of having autism. When a doctor tells a new mother that her child has autism, the doctor does not thereby inform her that her newborn child will be a morally worse person. Though they both suffer from emotional impairments, psychopaths are morally vicious and people with autism are not. This is because the psychopath's lack of emotion manifests an underlying lack of concern for others, while the lack of emotion in autistic people does not. Those with autism may have difficulty *understanding* whether or not they have hurt someone, but they often *care* deeply about not hurting others. Consider Stephanie Mayberry's description of her struggle with honesty:

> Many Aspies [people with Asperger's syndrome] tend to be very honest. You might think that that is a really good thing, but it has gotten me into trouble more than once. It has also caused me to hurt people's feelings, which is something I never, ever want to do.[51]

Stephanie is clearly concerned to avoid hurting other people's feelings but simply has trouble knowing when that will happen. In one study, for example, when asked about complex, social emotions, autistic children required more time, more prompts, and were more likely to resort to scripted responses than nonautistic children. They also used phrases like "I think" and "I guess" more often, suggesting they had to put in more cognitive effort.[52] If this is what underlies

---

51. Mayberry (2012, 432).
52. Capps et al. (1992, 1178ff.). This is also discussed in Losh and Capps (2006).

one's emotional impairment, it is a nonmoral, social vice—one simply finds it difficult to recognize or understand certain situations and their effects on others.

This also happens to nonautistics when they interact with a culture far removed from their own; they do something like stretch out their legs, buy a nice green hat for their newly married friend, or comfort a friend's father with a pat on the head.[53] One might even fail to understand the resulting expressions of hurt, misinterpreting pained laughter as genuine amusement or failing to grasp the meaning of a mortified gesture. Though others have been hurt, one might fail to experience social emotions like regret or embarrassment not because one doesn't *care*, but because one doesn't *understand* the meaning of the action or the other's response. In these situations one exhibits social vice, and perhaps cultural ignorance, but one is not a morally bad person.

Autistic people, because of their different experiences, often have this kind of empathetic blind spot. It's worth noting, however, that this works both ways. Temple Grandin describes a kind of sensory empathy that many nonautistics lack:

Normal people have an incredible lack of empathy. They have good emotional empathy, but they don't have much empathy for the autistic kid who is screaming at the baseball game because he can't stand the sensory overload. Or the autistic kid having a meltdown in the school cafeteria because there's too much stimulation. I'm frustrated with the inability of normal people to have sensory empathy. They can't seem to acknowledge these

53. In much of Southeast Asia, pointing your feet at something or someone important is offensive, as is touching someone's head (especially when that person is older or more important than you). In China, buying a married man a green hat implies that you are sleeping with his wife.

different realities because they're so far away from their own experiences.[54]

What comes through in this passage is that Temple cares about the suffering of others and values empathy for their suffering. She is also concerned with how few people are able to engage in sensory empathy. She even feels frustration about the situation—we can leave it open just how *emotional* this frustration is (perhaps it is simply a cold, intellectual judgment and a frustrated desire, or perhaps it is something more).

Though both psychopaths and autistic people generally lack certain emotions, there is a world of difference between them. Temple is so unlike the psychopath, whose emotional reaction to murder is likened to crushing a bug; she has, in fact, devoted her life to *reducing* animal suffering in slaughterhouses. Morally, the two are worlds apart because what is important for moral virtue is not having the right emotions or having the emotions that most humans have, but having the right cares and concerns.

Accounts that ground virtue in what is human miss this important distinction—psychopaths are vicious not because they are *inhuman*, because they lack certain distinctively human emotions, but because they are *inhumane*, they lack concern for others. The failure to feel *itself* is not morally vicious, only failing to feel *because one fails to care*. Whatever cognitive or affective defects Temple Grandin has, they do not include a lack of moral concern. In his reflections Oliver Sacks echoes this writing, "Temple is an intensely moral creature."[55] His diction is telling in two ways: "creature" suggests Temple lacks something that is found in most humans, but

54. Valentine and Hamilton (2006).
55. Sacks (1995, 296).

"moral" suggests that despite this, she *cares deeply* about morally important things.

VIRTUOUS IRRATIONAL EMOTIONS

If emotions are made virtuous or vicious by manifesting concern, then an emotion can be virtuous even when irrational, so long as it manifests moral concern—irrational emotions can be morally virtuous. This is in contrast with a number of views that require virtuous emotions to be rational. Historically, this view has been prominent among Stoics like Epictetus and Buddhists like Śāntideva.[56] It is also found in Aristotle and his followers, who argue that virtuous emotions must be in harmony with reason.[57] It is natural, at least for many philosophers, to think that virtuous emotions *must* be rational.

Of course, saying that an emotion is rational or in harmony with reason can mean many different things. It may mean that the emotion is based on true beliefs or representations about how the world is, that it responds appropriately to evidence, or that it must be directed toward properties that really are good. In what follows, I will reject the idea that virtuous emotions must be rational in all of these senses. An emotion, I will argue, can be morally virtuous without being rational in any of these ways.

---

56. Contrary to the common stereotype, Stoics do not advise eliminating *all* emotions. For example, they acknowledge joy, cheerfulness, and confidence as at least important for virtue—see Long (1996, 198). They do, however, advise eliminating *irrational* emotions, that is, emotions whose judgments misrepresent the world; see Epictetus' *Discourses* III.2.4, DeBrabander (2004, 202–203), and Long (1996, 209). Śāntideva argues in various ways that anger is vicious because it is unwarranted in his *Bodhicaryāvatāra* (especially VI.22ff); see Bommarito (2011) for an interpretation of these arguments.

57. See *NE* 1098a12–18. More recently, Hursthouse (1999, 116) takes virtue to entail a harmony between emotions and reason.

Allowing for virtuous, irrational emotions is a feature, not a bug of my account of virtuous and vicious emotion. After discussing some cases of virtuous irrationality found in previous work, I'll focus on two types of virtuous, irrational emotions: those that are irrational in their intensity, feeling a stronger emotion than the evidence warrants, and those that are irrational by overextension, feeling an emotion in the wrong situation or toward the wrong object.

On some views, virtuous emotions must accurately represent the world.[58] On this view, virtuous emotions need to get it right about how the world is; virtuous fear accurately represents how dangerous the object is, virtuous gratitude accurately represents benefits we have received, and so on. Feeling things as they are may be good in a variety of ways—it might, for example, be epistemically useful or beneficial for overall flourishing. It is not, however, a necessary condition for an emotion to count as morally virtuous.

An emotion that *erroneously* represents the world (whether rationally or irrationally) is not necessarily vicious and may even be virtuous. Ptolemy may have been overjoyed with his geocentric model of planetary motion and the mere fact that his joy involves a misrepresentation of reality does not reflect poorly on his moral character. Or consider someone who feels distress and agitation when seeing a child in the distance fall into a well. If such distress is in fact a manifestation of her concern for the safety of others, then it reflects well on her character *even if it was really only a log that fell into the well.* The fact that the aspect of her emotion that represents the world did so incorrectly does not change how the emotion involves a concern for others.

---

58. Ronald de Sousa, for example, claims that our most general emotional responsibility is to "feel things as they really are" (1990, 315).

Errors are one thing, but what about irrationality? Irrational emotions are not simply those that incorrectly represent the world but those that fail to respond appropriately to the available evidence. So if I resent my computer for deleting my work, my resentment is irrational because I have a lot of evidence that my computer is not an agent and could not delete my work on purpose. If I am afraid of napkins, my fear is irrational because I have a lot of evidence that napkins are not dangerous. There are many cases where irrational emotions seem not only nonvicious but positively virtuous.[59]

Consider a pair of virtues discussed by Julia Driver that involve irrationality: trust and blind charity. First, let's consider blind charity. The person with blind charity sees the good in others while ignoring the bad. More than that, such a person feels certain emotions toward others based on this charitable view: a warm fondness and admiration, for example. Driver's paradigm case of this virtue is Jane Bennet from Jane Austen's *Pride and Prejudice*, who, according to her sister Elizabeth is able "to take the good of everybody's character and make it still better, and say nothing of the bad."[60]

Blind charity involves irrationally mistreating evidence. Jane ignores, or at least downplays, bad events or character traits and accentuates good ones. It also involves emotional responses: Jane's charity involves feeling more acceptance, admiration, and fellowship with others and less hostility, bitterness, and revulsion toward them. Of course, taken to the extreme, this is naïveté. But Jane need not take things that far; she might simply massage the evidence to be slightly more favorable to others in a way that the ideally rational person

---

59. Tamar Szabó Gendler (2011) has argued that this is the case for belief; in many cases, our beliefs can be either rational or equitable, but not both. Refraining from prejudging people based on race or class may involve ignoring or failing to respond to previous evidence in ways that an ideally epistemically rational person would.
60. This is quoted in Driver (2001, 28).

would not. She need not be *grossly* irrational, simply less than ideally rational.

There does seem to be *something* good about someone who "gives others a break" in this way or who has the kind of optimistic emotional responses that Jane exhibits. An important part of why Jane's blind charity seems to reflect well on her is that it manifests her concern for others. It is easy to think your own child's drawing is better than it really is or to take the crazy idea of a close friend more seriously than you should. This is because our care and closeness affect our responses in ways that make us more charitable. Jane's charity is like this, but applied to everyone—her charity manifests a closeness and concern for everyone she meets. This is not to say that her charity is rational, rather that it reflects well on her *despite* being irrational.

The other virtue of this kind is a type of trust. Not all trust involves the irrational treatment of evidence. Often we trust someone based on evidence like their track record and the testimony of others, as when one hires a security guard based on their job history and references. Other cases of trust, however, are not sensitive to evidence and can even run counter to the evidence.

Consider a case offered by Driver.[61] Brenda's close friend has been accused of a crime and despite strong evidence to the contrary, her friend insists on her innocence. Despite this evidence, Brenda trusts her friend. Brenda doesn't deny the evidence; when asked, she can admit that the evidence does in fact suggest that her friend is guilty. Nevertheless, she sticks by her friend, trusting in her innocence *despite* this evidence. Whether or not this trust itself is an emotional response, Brenda will likely feel a variety of

---

61. Driver (2001, 30–31). She draws on what Judith Baker (1987) calls "special" trust or "friendship" trust.

associated emotions: She may feel dejected, troubled, or tense over her friend's predicament. She may feel indignation toward the police or a stronger feeling of closeness with her friend. These responses all involve representing her friend as innocent, despite the evidence to the contrary.

It's important to keep in mind that Brenda need not trust in her friend until the end, against *all possible evidence*. To count as irrational, she simply has to respond to the evidence differently than how an ideally rational person would respond. To count as irrationally trusting her friend, Brenda need not insist on her innocence come what may, but simply require more evidence than an impartial, ideally rational observer would. If this is the case, Brenda's trust in her friend and many of its associated emotions reflect well on her, even though it is not how an ideally rational person would respond. Brenda's emotions are both irrational and virtuous. Her emotions respond to evidence about how the world is in a less-than-ideal way; nevertheless, they manifest loyalty and concern for her friend.

If your taste in virtue includes the theological, trust is similar to a virtue from the Christian tradition: faith. Though Aquinas defines the virtue as intellectual, it can also involve a constellation of emotional responses.[62] Though its roots are in a theological context, it can occur in nonreligious contexts, too; we can have faith in our friends, the democratic system, or the kindness of strangers. When these are epistemically insensitive, the emotions are similar to the "optimism of the will and pessimism of the intellect" that many have taken to be virtuous.[63] In this case, however, it involves an irrational optimism of the emotions, despite a realism of the intellect. That

---

62. Aquinas defines it as "a habit of the mind, whereby eternal life is begun in us, making the intellect assent to what is non-apparent." See *Summa*, Part II Q.4.
63. This is most often attributed to Antonio Gramsci or Romain Rolland.

is, one may intellectually recognize evidence but nevertheless have emotional reactions that represent the world in a way insensitive to that evidence. These irrational emotions can still manifest morally important cares and concerns and can still reflect well on one's character.

Driver's explanation for why blind charity or trust can be virtuous is that such traits, in general, lead to good results. This may be a good feature of these traits, but it is not what makes them virtuous. Brenda's trust, for example, reflects well on her even if it leads her (and others like her) to stick by bad friends slightly longer than they should, resulting in more pain than if they were less trusting. More importantly, what underlying attitude these emotional responses manifest makes a difference to whether or not they are virtuous. If Brenda's trust in her friend manifests that she cares deeply about those around her, it reflects well on her. If, however, it manifests a concern to rebel against her rule-worshipping father, then it is not. Both of these may produce the same effects, but the former reflects something good about Brenda in a way that the latter does not.

There are other ways that irrational emotions can be virtuous. We often take small irrationalities to reflect well on someone's character. Suppose you're about to take a long trip and, though you are traveling far away, you know very well that the trip is not a dangerous one and there is no reason to be worried about your safety. Now suppose you tell a loved one this and their reply is a calm and unfazed, "Okay, I'm not worried." You might find yourself thinking, "You're not *even a little bit* worried?!"[64] It can be nice for a loved one to be a little bit more worried than the evidence warrants because such worry shows how much they care about you and your safety.

---

64. Thanks to Nomy Arpaly for this example.

Similar cases can happen over more explicitly moral issues. It can reflect well on someone when they feel slightly more guilt or remorse over breaking a trivial promise than is warranted. If their disproportionate guilt is a manifestation of just how much keeping promises matters to them, it reflects well on their character. Such irrationalities are not *always* virtuous. If they are not a manifestation of more general morally good concerns, they will not be virtuous: If someone feels more guilt over an inconsequential broken promise than the evidence warrants because they are drunk or because it helps them avoid thinking about their ongoing divorce, then it is not virtuous.

Emotions can also be virtuous even when irrationally directed toward improper objects. A friend once confided to me that she couldn't help but feel bad for a spoon separated from its set or a damaged doll that nobody wanted to buy. A spoon cannot feel left out; dolls cannot feel rejected or unloved. Having sympathy toward them is irrational. Still, when my friend told me this, I couldn't help but feel that it said *something* good about her. But why?

It can't be because such emotions manifest morally important concern; a doll does not have well-being. There is nothing morally good about caring about a spoon's alleged well-being. Instead, these feelings are virtuous by manifesting a more general morally good concern. My friend's irrational sympathy reflects well on her because it manifested a more general, morally good concern: Care for those who are in some way damaged and as a result are ignored and undervalued. This kind of care is not only morally good but incredibly rare and very difficult to maintain. Her sympathy manifests this more general and morally valuable concern, which gets overextended from damaged people to damaged dolls. When a person's concerns misfire in this way, by being extended beyond their relevant objects, it still shows that the person has such morally good concerns. It also can show that such concerns are easily and readily manifested, even if this results in manifesting as irrational emotion.

There are also, of course, cases where such emotions do not manifest a more general concern. If such emotions manifest a narrow predilection rather than more general moral concern, then it is not virtuous. There is, for example, nothing virtuous about a Nazi who feels bad for an orphaned spoon, but not an orphaned Jewish girl. To count as virtuous, they must be overextensions of genuinely valuable moral concerns rather than a localized psychological reaction.

In practice this can be difficult to distinguish. Many hoarders, for example, experience strong moral emotions toward personified objects. For example, consider one hoarder's description of her experience throwing away an empty yogurt container:

> I remember feeling bad about not choosing "this" particular container as one that would remain at home with the others, and so I was feeling responsible for rejecting it and placing it into the recycling bin to begin its long journey to eventual destruction. I felt responsible for giving it as "comfortable" a ride as possible, seeing as how I was rejecting it, and the thought of it having to endure a humid, long journey made me very anxious. This was followed quickly by the thought of how silly this thinking was, and that I needed to resist following through on what I wanted to do to make me feel less anxious.[65]

Are these emotions also morally virtuous? It is unclear to what extent these emotions are merely compulsive tics and to what extent they manifest her more general moral concerns. Though one

65. Frost and Steketee (2010, 273).

gets the feeling that her emotions are similar to an itch, a simple and blind urge, the language she uses, talk of responsibility and comfort, makes it seem too complex and too moralized to be *completely* independent of her cares.

It is most likely a mix of the two. Her disorder is tic-like in the sense that it compels her to have *some* strong emotion about *something*, but it is still directed to some extent by her cares and concerns. Her emotions are like a bright light that is filtered through the prism of her cares and concerns. That is why she has *these particular* feelings about the yogurt container.

Again, even if her emotions do manifest a concern, the immediate concern it manifests is not morally good. The concern for the "comfort" and "well-being" of a yogurt container *itself* is not morally virtuous—Caring about plastic bottles, even when personified, is not a morally important care. Her emotions can, however, also manifest a more general concern that *is* morally relevant. In this case, the irrational emotions seem to say *something* about her more general cares and concerns: She is concerned with providing comfort, acceptance, and taking responsibility—all morally important notions.

Of course, the hoarder's overall life quality might be better if she lacked such emotions and she would be wise to attempt to focus her concern only on the appropriate objects. But if her emotions are the irrational overextension of morally good concerns, then such manifestations count in favor of her moral character (though perhaps only to a very small degree).

This explains why she seems to be a better person (albeit only *slightly* better) than another compulsive hoarder who feels anxiety when he fails to torture, abandon, and hurt yogurt containers. Insofar as the hoarder's emotions manifest, at least partially, more general concerns that are morally important, such irrational emotions can be (at least *slightly*) virtuous or vicious.

Insofar as her emotions are slightly virtuous, it is not because the associated behaviors are morally *good*. There is, after all, nothing morally good about helping a yogurt container; the action itself is morally neutral. It can, however, be morally *virtuous* if it manifests a more general morally good concern. It is also important to note that her attitudes can be virtuous even if she never expresses them and does not act on them in an overt way. Most people who feel bad about a damaged doll or an abandoned spoon because of more general moral concern never act on such feelings and may never express them to anyone.

None of this is to say that we should all try to become less rational. I've only argued that an emotion being irrational is *compatible* with its being virtuous. That is, an emotion may be bad in some respects, say prudentially or rationally, and yet still reflect well on one's moral character. There are reasons to avoid having irrational emotions, but not because they will make you *morally* vicious.

These emotions are good, but not in a way that is to be pursued or promoted. It may sound strange to think that there can be goods that are not to be promoted; isn't it part of the meaning of calling something "good" that one wants to promote it? Not always. Think of how Kantians describe moral worth. Kant rightly pointed out that there is something *good* about having a strong desire to hit someone but overcoming that desire and not acting on it. This does not mean that we should all cultivate the desire to hit others just so we can overcome it. Many things are good in this way: It is good to be brave in battle, but that doesn't mean we should start more wars so that more people can be brave. It is good to quit smoking, but that does not mean nonsmokers should start smoking just so more people can quit. Irrational emotions are like this—there is something genuinely good about them, but that does not mean we should make ourselves less rational to maximize this good.

CONCLUSION

Emotions can be relevant to moral character independently of any associated overt behaviors; even when unable to be expressed outwardly, emotions can manifest moral concern. A wide variety of emotions are open to creatures like Weather Watchers or those with locked-in syndrome: Despite being unable to act, a Weather Watcher can feel anxious about a fellow Weather Watcher who is in danger, sympathy when they are hurt, and relief when they recover. Someone with locked-in syndrome can feel racial disgust, indignation over political events, or gratitude toward those that help them. Though they are unable to express or act on these emotions, they are still relevant to their moral character.

When emotions are virtuous, it is not because they are rational or are distinctly human. They are ways one's underlying moral concerns manifest in the emotional realm. Despite this, particular emotions are not necessary for being a good person. One may lack certain emotions for reasons having nothing to do with one's moral care or concern. These include cognitive disorders like autism or various medications but also matters of personality, temperament, and culture.

Virtuous people in different cultures will have different emotional responses. This is partly because some emotions are only possible in a certain cultural context: One cannot experience Catholic guilt without being brought up in a specific moral, metaphysical, and theological culture. Someone in a culture with dramatically different expectations about how a life story should go cannot experience the particular combination of emotions that make up a midlife crisis.

Again, my focus has been on moral character. Having an emotional deficit may make your life go worse, flourish less, or be less pleasurable. It need not, however, make you a morally worse person. Such people may be missing something of value in life, and it can be tempting to say that they're not living a full life. But it's worth noting that missing value in life is incredibly easy. I do not have perfect pitch, and cannot see ultraviolet light. I'm illiterate in thousands of languages. These things cut me off from a lot of value in the world, but they do not prevent me from living a full or happy life.

These issues are complex, but it is also worth noting that whether or not certain traits allow for a full or happy life depends, at least in part, on social facts. Being black in a racist area or being gay at almost any point in the past made it difficult to live a happy and full life. This is not because there is anything bad about being black or gay, but because of how society is organized. If we imagine a world where the kind of sensory sensitivity that people with autism often have is prized and social emotions aren't, our opinions about what sensitivities are necessary for a full and happy life might be very different.

Though there may be general emotional families that are more or less universal, *particular* emotions within these families can require particular situations and so will be less universal in nature.[66] Many of these, like spousal love or filial piety, can be virtuous even though there are cultures without the family units or marriage customs those emotions depend on. Someone is not a worse person for lacking these emotions simply because they are from a society with a different social and cultural structure.

---

66. Talk of basic or universal emotions presumes that humans are, to *some* extent, deeply similar. This similarity will be described in different ways depending on one's academic allegiances: Someone influenced by natural science will explain that humans share "fundamental life-tasks" (Ekman 1992b, 171), while someone more rooted in the humanities will refer to "the human condition" (Solomon 2007, 248). The idea is the same: People everywhere share both biological similarities and situational challenges and triumphs; we all suffer loss, relate to others, achieve aims, and face dangers.

Perhaps most importantly, this allows for morally irrelevant variation in emotional responses. Virtuous people need not be emotional clones of one another. Having a calm temperament and being pessimistic are not moral defects; they don't make you a morally worse person. If someone's righteous indignation, admiration, or gratitude manifests their moral concern, it reflects well on them. If someone else has that same depth of concern but fails to feel such things because they are calm by nature, that person is not morally worse.

This does not, however, mean that it is always misguided to say things such as "You should be less angry than you are" or "You should feel less gratitude for what she did." This "should" can be meant in a variety of senses. It might be practical; perhaps someone should feel less anger because it is destructive and making them unhappy. Or it might be rational; perhaps someone should feel more gratitude because it would be warranted. When thinking about how an emotion reflects on someone's moral character, however, what matters is not how angry or grateful they are; after all, this can be affected by a variety of factors unrelated to moral character. What we really respond to when we think someone has insufficiently intense emotions is a presumed lack of concern because a lack of emotion *in general* manifests a lack of concern.

I've given an answer to the question: *When are emotions morally virtuous and why?* I have not attempted to answer the question: *How emotional will a virtuous person be?* This is because the latter question is a question without an answer. It is like asking, "How colorful will a beautiful painting be?" Just as two paintings using different color palettes can be equally beautiful, two people with different emotional ranges can be equally virtuous. Some paintings are beautiful with very little color and others are beautiful by being very colorful. Even though, in the colorful painting, the colors are part of the beauty, less colorful paintings are not less beautiful simply because they lack those particular colors. Even though a highly emotional virtuous person's emotions are part of what makes them virtuous, a less emotional person is not thereby less virtuous simply by lacking those particular emotions.

Seeing emotions as virtuous by manifesting moral concern allows for this variation between virtuous people with different personalities and from different cultures. At the same time, it explains what they all share that makes them virtuous—they all share an underlying concern for moral goods. They all care about things like the rights and well-being of others. This does not mean that they have identical inner lives; what they share is deep concern for moral goods. What makes them virtuous is what they care about, what matters to them.

Chapter 5

Attention

Consider an increasingly common scene in modern life. In the middle of an important conversation with a friend, you notice something change. Their eyes slowly drift downward, toward something in their hands just out of sight. They seem to hear your voice still, but you can tell that they aren't really listening anymore. Of course, you know by now that they're looking at their smartphone. Finding yourself in this situation can make you frustrated and a little offended. Why? Part of the answer, I think, is that your friend's lack of attention is a way of insufficiently valuing both you as a conversational partner and the importance of what you are saying. This is especially salient if you happen to be talking about something that's very important to you. You rightly feel as though your friend doesn't value what you are saying because of their lack of attention.

We expect a virtuous person to have certain habits of attention; they will attend to certain things and ignore others. They will, for example, tend to notice when people around them are in pain and pay attention to the benefits that others provide. Though this book has focused on moral evaluations of people, we might think that a virtuous person wouldn't devote much of their attention to sizing up others or dwelling on how virtuous they are. These patterns of attention, I'll argue, are virtuous because they manifest morally important cares and concerns.

Sometimes these habits of attention will be expressed in action, as when a friend looks at their phone while talking to you, but other times they will remain as inner states, as when your mind secretly wanders during a lecture. After a brief overview of attention, I will argue that attention (and inattention) can be morally virtuous or vicious. This is not, as others have claimed, because attention *itself* has moral value, but because attention is a way of manifesting moral concern. This best explains why not all failures of attention are vicious and also the importance of attention in traditional virtues like gratitude and modesty.

WHAT IS ATTENTION?

Suppose that one sunny day a philosopher, let's call her Emma, is walking through campus and thinking very hard about the main argument of a paper she is writing. Completely focused on working out her argument, she walks around a tree that was in her path. She was not ignorant of the tree; she did, after all, manage to avoid walking into it. At the same time, she did not pay attention to the tree—her attention was entirely focused on the argument she was working out.[1] Emma's case is a simple one that illustrates the difference between awareness and attention. Emma was *aware* of the tree despite not paying any *attention* to it. One can be aware of something, can be able to respond to it, without it appearing in our conscious, reflective mind.

---

1. Thanks to Nomy Arpaly and Tim Schroeder for this example. A similar distinction can be found in Velleman (2013).

Attention is a complex and multifaceted phenomenon. Here, I will use "attention" to refer to a focusing or directing of the conscious mind toward an object; it is a way the conscious mind is directed or captured. This idea has its origins in an oft-cited passage from the *Principles of Psychology* by William James:

> Everyone knows what attention is. It is the taking possession by the mind, in clear and vivid form, of one out of what seem several simultaneously possible objects or trains of thought. Focalization, concentration, of consciousness are of its essence. It implies withdrawal from some things in order to deal effectively with others.[2]

James's description simplifies things in many ways, but it offers a good starting point. The idea that attention involves directed consciousness is common in contemporary cognitive science on the subject.[3] To attend to something is to notice it, for it to be salient in one's conscious experience.[4]

---

2. James (1890/2007, 403).

3. For example, Koch (2004, 163ff.) notes that most psychologists take attention and consciousness to be deeply linked. Stazicker (2011) talks of "focusing" or "concentrating" our consciousness on an object, and Watzl (2011) describes it as a "structuring of the stream of consciousness." An exception here is Prinz (2011, 90ff.), who takes attention to be a process that makes information available to working memory.

4. Wayne Wu, for example, describes it as "phenomenal salience," noting that when we attend to an object, "the attended object is experienced as highlighted, accentuated, spotlighted, emphasized or more salient in contrast to unattended objects concurrently perceived" (2011a, 94). Some object to the use of the spotlight metaphor when discussing attention. Like all metaphors, its accuracy depends largely on what the relevant similarities are supposed to be. Block (2010) highlights some of the weaknesses of the spotlight metaphor when applied to visual attention by noting that there can be multiple "fields" of visual attention with vague size and shape. Attention is not like a spotlight in *every* sense; those who find the metaphor confusing or misleading may ignore it.

Most important for the current discussion, attention does not require overt action and can be involuntary. Visual attention is often associated with particular eye movement, but the two can come apart: We can distinguish overt attention, which involves bodily movement, from covert attention, which does not. It is possible to focus your gaze on an object, while paying attention to an object in your peripheral vision. Think of times when you try to determine if the person at the next table in a restaurant is an old acquaintance or not. Accomplishing this without making the person uncomfortable requires attending to their face while keeping your gaze fixed on the people at your own table.[5]

This is especially clear in cases of nonvisual attention. We do not need to move our bodies in order to attend to the phrasing of a melody or to the sound of a distant birdcall. We can also attend to physical sensations, such as an annoying itch or the pain of a migraine, without moving our bodies. There is also attention to inner mental events, as when Emma attends to an argument, when someone thinks about a riddle, or consciously replays an event from the day before. Though there can be overt actions that are generally associated with these kinds of attention, they are not requirements of attending.[6]

This attention is sometimes voluntary and sometimes involuntary. Sometimes it is something we *do*, and other times something

---

5. For more on the distinction between gaze and attention, see Posner (1980) and the discussion in Prinz (2011, 114).

6. Allport takes attention to require "the subject's ability to act voluntarily" (1987, 414); this is developed into a stronger claim by Wu (2014), who takes attention to be selection for action. This may seem to be in tension with my claims, but it is important to note that Wu distinguishes attention from other states like perception, memory, and conscious thinking in a way that I do not, suggesting he is concerned with a more narrow mental phenomenon. It is also important to note that Wu includes among the actions that attention selects for, *covert* mental actions like deliberating, imagining, recalling, and thinking; see Wu (2011b).

that *happens* to us. We can deliberately attend to the combination of flavors in a Scotch, what time it currently is, or what that awful smell is. Though it can be a voluntary action, it need not be an overt, behavioral one. You can, for example, pay attention to someone at a party while *acting* as if you are ignoring them. A skilled slacker can act as if they are paying attention in class, even though they're completely focused on determining which bar to go to later that night. Even when attention is voluntary, it is often a private, mental action.

Our attention can also be involuntarily grabbed, regardless of our will: by a sudden crack of thunder, the brightly colored billboard with a bikini-clad girl, or the sound of a familiar song. Our attention can be a voluntary, mental action or an involuntary mental event.[7] While my account will explain how both voluntary and involuntary attention can be morally virtuous or vicious, it is important to keep in mind that attention is often involuntary.

Attention also has duration; it is a state that persists through time. In addition to the local state, I will discuss broader patterns of attention. Being attentive or inattentive in this broader sense involves patterns of localized attention: Someone who is currently distracted can still be an attentive spouse because of a more general pattern of attention. Someone who dwells too much on his previous business failures may, at the moment, be engrossed in a movie. Sometimes dwelling is vicious even though a single episode of

---

7. Works influenced by cognitive science often discuss "top-down" and "bottom-up" attention, referring to the order of mental processing—see Prinz (2011, 94ff.) and Koch (2004, 162). Cognitive scientists also distinguish between exogenous (initiated by external stimuli) and endogenous (initiated by internal states) attention. Wu (2014, 29ff.) gives a clear discussion distinguishing top-down/bottom-up, controlled/automatic, and voluntary/involuntary types of attention. My discussion will not rely on such fine distinctions, simply on the claims that attention *can* be involuntary and that not all involuntary attention is independent from our cares and concerns.

attention is not, as I will argue is the case with modesty. Sometimes attending is virtuous, but dwelling is not, as in cases of scrupulosity.

Attention, as I will use it, is primarily a way of directing our conscious minds toward some objects and away from others, as when Emma attends to her argument but not to the tree in her path. This may be voluntary, as when I decide to attend to the weather outside my window, or involuntary, as when a loud bang grabs my attention. In either case, it does not require overt behaviors, though they may be associated with attention in general.

ETHICS AND ATTENTION: THE DEFECTIVE AND THE VICIOUS

Though rarely discussed explicitly in much work in moral philosophy, some have taken attention itself to be morally virtuous. Simone Weil, for example, makes attention central in her ethics. However, she uses the term in a more technical and idiosyncratic sense. For her it is a kind of mystical, loving, and selfless observation.[8] This technical sense of the term is also used by Iris Murdoch. Explicitly drawing on Weil's use, she takes it to be a "just and loving gaze" that is itself morally good.[9]

Murdoch and Weil, though they take this specialized attention to itself be valuable, also highlight its importance in moral

---

8. Siân Miles describes it as "a form of stepping back from all roles, including that of observer. It is a distancing of one's self not only from the thing observed, but from one's own faculties of observation" (1986, 8). Weil writes in a way that makes clear she is not using the term in the ordinary sense: "Attention, taken to its highest degree, is the same thing as prayer. It presupposes faith and love" (1947/1999, 170).

9. Murdoch writes, "I have used the word 'attention', which I borrow from Simone Weil, to express the idea of a just and loving gaze directed upon an individual reality" (1964/2001, 33). Mole (2007, 83) discusses how, for her, this attention is itself a bearer of value.

development and in producing right action. Both claim that attention itself is sufficient to produce moral action and moral development.[10] Part of what allows them to make these claims is a concept of attention that is far more robust, one that is, by definition, loving and just.

Though I employ a far less moralized notion of attention than the one used by Weil and Murdoch, my aim will be to show how even this more sparse attention can be morally virtuous, not because it has intrinsic moral value itself, but because it can have a deep connection with our cares and concerns.

Attention in the sense that I am using the term, as a way of directing one's conscious mind, seems to be morally neutral. Deep attention to someone, "really looking" as Murdoch might say, is not always morally virtuous. Robert Hare, describes the kind of close attention that psychopaths often exhibit: "when psychopaths see grotesque images of blown-apart faces, they aren't horrified. They're *absorbed.*"[11] This close attention does not make the psychopath morally better. It also need not produce good actions; no amount of attending to a person in need will make a thoroughly cruel person motivated to help.

It is not only psychopaths that can have this kind of attention. Someone who thinks "morality is for wimps" may frequently attend to acts of generosity and still feel only revulsion and contempt—prolonged attention may even reinforce these reactions. In group situations, both kids and adults often pay close attention to an outsider, looking for psychological weak spots, so they can best

---

10. For example, Weil writes, "If we turn our minds towards the good, it is impossible that little by little the whole soul will not be attracted thereto in spite of itself" (1947/1999, 117). Murdoch echoes this claiming, "Where virtue is concerned we often apprehend more than we clearly understand and *grow by looking*" (1964/2001, 30). Emphasis in original.

11. Quoted in Ronson (2011, 95). Emphasis in original.

mock and intimidate them. A con artist may need to "really look" at someone, to see their habits, fears, and desires, in order to better trick them.

Some have argued that attention in the ordinary, nonmoralized sense can *itself* be virtuous or vicious. Consider an example by Lawrence Blum contrasting John and Joan's different attentive responses to someone in pain:

> John, let us say, often fails to take in people's discomfort, whereas Joan is characteristically sensitive to such discomfort. It is thus in character for the discomfort [of another person] to be salient for Joan but not for John. That is to say, a morally significant aspect of situations facing John characteristically fails to be salient for him, and this is a defect in his character—not a very serious moral defect, but a defect nevertheless. John misses something of the moral reality confronting him.[12]

The idea here is that some failures of attention *themselves* are morally vicious. John's failure to notice other people's discomfort makes him vicious. Because a morally significant feature often fails to be salient to him, fails to capture his attention, he is morally worse. The fact that his attention misses something of the moral reality gives him a moral defect.

The use of "defect" here is not simply a charming euphemism for moral vice; it masks an important distinction between simple mistakes, cognitive or perceptual failures, and moral vice. All moral vices may be defects, but not all defects are moral vices. Being clumsy, bad at mental math, or diabetic are all kinds of defects, but

---

12. Blum (1994, 33); he continues in a footnote writing, "The failure of perception can be significant in its own right" (1994, 33fn.6).

none of them are morally vicious. One is not a morally worse person for being diabetic or clumsy. This is because such traits do not reveal anything about what matters to them, what they care about.[13]

When disconnected from our cares and concerns, defective attention is not vicious but merely defective—it does not say anything about one's moral character. Consider the idea that John's failure of perception is *itself* morally significant. Now suppose we learn that John is blind. Is his perceptual failure still morally significant? It clearly is not; one is not a morally worse person simply because one is blind. But this can be hard to explain if one takes attention *itself* to be virtuous. After all, someone who is blind still, in Blum's words, "misses something of the moral reality." A blind person's failure to attend to the discomfort of another is not morally vicious. It is a defect of the eyes, not of the spirit. It says nothing about the person's cares or concerns, nothing about their moral character.

Or suppose that John can see but has untreated attention-deficit disorder (ADD). A central symptom of ADD is an inability to focus and maintain attention. People who suffer from ADD have difficulty not only sustaining attention but also filtering irrelevant information and directing attention.[14] Those with ADD have an attentional defect; their perception does not function correctly. And yet one is not a morally worse person simply in virtue of having ADD. Why not?

The answer, I think, is that the kind of defective attention associated with ADD is disconnected from one's cares and concerns. The

---

13. I am in disagreement here not just with Blum but also Adams (2006, 104ff.), who claims that there are purely cognitive moral vices that are independent of desires (which would fall under what I call concern) and Aristotelians who take failures to perform aspects of a distinctive human function to be morally vicious.

14. See Whiteman and Novotni (1995, 119ff.) and Young and Bramham (2007, 59ff.). The exact cause is not known, but research suggests that it is a result of an imbalance of neurotransmitters, which help to transmit signals between cells—see Wender (2001, 35ff.).

inattention of someone with ADD does not manifest a lack of concern, but an inability to attend to what one takes to be important. This is a significant part of why the disorder is so intensely frustrating; one is unable to focus on the presentation that matters for the success of their new business or the conversation that could save the marriage they desperately want to save. Someone with ADD can care deeply about performing well on a test but be unable to focus their attention on the problem in front of them *despite* the exam being very important to them.[15]

If John has ADD and, having run out of medication, has a hard time keeping his attention from wandering where it will, his failure to attend to the person in discomfort is not vicious. His inattention does not mean he doesn't *care* about the well-being of others; it means his brain has a wiring problem that makes him unable to attend to what he *does* care about (moral or otherwise).

A failure to notice the discomfort in a neighboring person on a train is vicious if the inattention is a result of not caring for others, not if it is a result of a splitting headache. Similarly, a psychopath whose attention is captured by a person writhing in pain on the sidewalk because of a morbid curiosity does not exhibit a slight moral virtue nor does the thief who notices such a person because he is constantly on the lookout for an easy target.

Some philosophers, like Weil and Murdoch, get attention to be morally virtuous by building moral concern into the very concept. In doing this, however, one is unable to distinguish vicious failures of attention from nonvicious ones. By explaining virtuous and vicious attention by its connection to our moral cares and concerns, we can properly distinguish mere cognitive defects and bodily disabilities

---

15. See Taylor (2007, 7–13) for a first-hand account of this case. See also Young and Bramham (2007, 179).

from genuine moral vice. To do this, I will first argue that attention can be, and often is, connected with our cares and concerns.

ATTENTION AND CONCERN

Attention is often intimately related to care, and even love. When we love someone, when we care deeply about them, our attention is drawn to them; this is present in several philosophical discussions of love.[16] The clearest expression, however, is in a classic song:

> My love must be a kind of blind love
> I can't see anyone but you
> Are the stars out tonight?
> I don't know if it's cloudy or bright
> I only have eyes for you, dear
> I don't know if we're in a garden
> Or on a crowded avenue
> You are here and so am I
> Maybe millions of people go by
> But they all disappear from view
> And I only have eyes for you[17]

The singer "only has eyes" for his beloved, but this is not simply an ocular disorder; it is, after all, a love song. His attention is captured because of his feelings for her. This focused attention is not just a

16. See Swanton (2003, 34ff.) and Frankfurt (2006, 79). Noddings (1984/2003, esp. 24ff.) also makes relevant claims in her discussion of the role of engrossment in caring for someone. Ganeri (2017) defends an interpretation of Buddhaghosa that makes attention central for various aspects of moral life.
17. Composed by Harry Warren and lyricist Al Dubin, "I Only Have Eyes for You" was written for the 1934 film *Dames*. The definitive version was recorded by The Flamingos in 1959.

sign of his love; it is one way in which it manifests. This is not only a feature of romantic care: Caring parents tend to be attentive parents; they take photos and tell stories about their own children (and not the children living down the street). Caring advisors listen to (not just hear!) their students and notice if they are not around. A caring friend is, among other things, one for whom out of sight does not mean out of mind.

The idea that our concerns affect our attention is not a new one. The Chinese philosopher Liezi describes a greedy man who snatched gold pieces from a market shop in plain view of many bystanders. When the police caught him, they asked him why he tried to steal the gold in front of so many witnesses. He replied, "When I took it, I didn't see the people, only the gold." His excessive concern for gold, at least in that moment, made him unable to notice anything else.

Attention is intimately connected with what matters to us. Unlike the kind of care associated with care-based theories of ethics, which is generally limited to persons, attention manifests a much broader range of cares. It can, for example, manifest more abstract and impersonal concerns, too: A music lover will pay attention to what song is playing during a party and a linguist with a love of phonology will pay attention to how different people pronounce certain vowel sounds. Their care about these abstract topics manifests as attention.

It's no coincidence that our minds tend to wander during lectures on topics we don't care about. During these lectures, when the discussion shifts to something we *do* care about, it quickly captures our attention. This is a common phenomenon among students, noticed over a hundred years ago by William James:

> Not far removed is the talent which mind-wandering school-boys display during the hours of instruction, of noticing every

movement in which the teacher tells a story. I remember classes in which, instruction being uninteresting, and discipline relaxed, a buzzing murmur was always to be heard, which invariably stopped for as long a time as an anecdote lasted.[18]

Students care about anecdotes, not boring old *instruction*, so they converse during the lecture until the good part draws their attention. Their involuntary habits of conscious attention are closely connected to what they care about.

There are empirical data to support the idea that our concerns affect our attention. One study tested attention by asking subjects to focus on a plus sign at the center of their visual field and flashed different images in the subjects' peripheral vision.[19] Some images captured the subject's attention while others did not. Researchers found that a subject's own name grabs attention while other names do not, and images of happy faces attract attention whereas neutral and upside-down faces do not. It is not only positive things that attract attention; the word "rape" grabs attention in a way that the word "pear" does not, and swastikas attract attention in ways that less meaningful symbols don't. This result has also been found to work with auditory attention; when aurally distracted, subjects notice the sound of their own name more easily than other names.[20]

Of course, attention is not *always* connected with our concerns. Loud noises, bright colors, and strong smells can capture our attention regardless of what we care about. Someone on vacation in China who knows only a few Chinese characters will notice those characters on signs not because of any concern for what the characters

18. James (1892/1992, 215).
19. Mack and Rock (1998).
20. Moray (1959).

mean, but simply because they are recognizable. In rural Nepal, for example, some people cross dangerous rope bridges so often that they no longer give a second thought to the danger involved. This isn't because they don't care about danger, but because they are used to it and so no longer pay much attention to it.

Attention can also be affected by our previous cognitive states and our level of skill in various tasks. When we first learn to drive, we must pay close attention to various aspects of the task ("More gas! Less clutch! Check your blind spot!"). As we develop the relevant motor skills and mental habits, these things no longer demand our conscious attention, even though we care just as much about them as when we first started. This feature of attention need not involve overt action: A beginning logic student may need to attend closely to the operators of a sentence in formal logic to determine if it is truth-functionally true, while an experienced logician need not attend to each operator.

In addition to skill, our attention is also sometimes affected by what we already happen to believe, though in complex ways. Sometimes this is simply confirmation bias: People can overattend to evidence that supports what they already believe and fail to attend to rival explanations for the same evidence. Research shows that this happens in a variety of situations, from working out logic puzzles, to evaluating personality characterizations, to assessing the predictions of psychics.[21] This often has little if anything to do with

---

21. See Baron (2007, 186ff.) for a summary of research on attentional bias and Nickerson (1998, 177ff.) for research on its role in confirmation bias. This can happen in the opposite way, too: We can sometimes also overattend to evidence *against* what we already believe so that we can better undermine it and explain it away. See Gilovich (1991), especially the chapter entitled "Seeing What We Expect to See," and Kelly (2008, 617ff.) for a discussion of this phenomenon. What is important for me is that in both cases, our prior beliefs affect our patterns of attention.

our cares: Someone can idly form a hypothesis about a probability puzzle and then overattend to cases that support it, even though they care very little about what the answer to the puzzle is or even about getting it right. Sometimes overattending to correlations or to evidence may be a purely cognitive matter, the result of using efficient heuristics in making judgments.[22]

Though our patterns of attention can be the result of cognitive heuristics that are independent of our cares and concerns, this is not *always* the case. Our attentional habits are also the result of what we care about: A woman who cares about being her father's favorite daughter will likely overattend to instances where her father favored her over her sister.[23] A Christian who cares about the efficacy of prayer will likely overattend to cases where their prayers seemed to be answered and ignore cases where they prayed and nothing happened.

My account of how attention can be virtuous or vicious will not require that attention *always* manifests what we care about, only that it *can*. In the same way that birdwatchers will notice the birds on a walk because they care about birds and structural engineers will notice the support beams in a building because they care about architectural design, morally virtuous people will notice much about the world because they care about moral goods.

VIRTUOUS AND VICIOUS ATTENTION

Recall the example where Joan attends to someone in pain and John does not. When would Joan's attention reflect well on her moral character, and when would John's lack of attention reflect poorly on

---

22. Many of the heuristics and biases described are in the work of Daniel Kahneman and Amos Tversky. See, for example, Tversky and Kahneman (1974).
23. Mele (2001) gives this and similar examples in his discussion of self-deception.

his? The best explanation is one that appeals to the underlying cares or concerns that their attention manifests: Joan's attention is virtuous if it manifests concern for the distressed person and not if she is simply bored or notices because she always gets a good laugh when she sees someone else suffering. John's failure to attend only reflects poorly on him if it manifests a lack of concern for the person in pain, not if he is blind or sleep deprived and unable to focus on anything very well.

Attention can manifest our concerns and, when those concerns are moral, the attention is virtuous—it says something about what matters to us. This sounds big, but it can show itself in small ways. My attention to a stranger's sniffle on the bus can manifest a concern for *my own* health ("I *do not* have time to get sick this week!") or a concern for *his* health ("That guy doesn't sound too good; I hope he feels better soon").

Or consider the vicious attention attributed to the stereotypical mafia wife. The mafia wife pays a lot of attention to the expensive gifts given to her by her gangster husband, but she ignores the source of such gifts. Her attention betrays a concern for nice things, but a lack of concern for the cruelty and misdeeds that make them possible. Such attention manifests moral indifference, even if there is nothing she can do to change the situation. Many middle-class North Americans exhibit, to some degree, the same attention pattern. We pay attention to the stylish new electronics or the great deal we got on a new pair of jeans, but pay little attention to the exploitation and injustice that make such things possible. To the extent that this reveals a deeper concern for electronic novelty than for justice and human rights, this inattention is vicious.

It might seem that such attention is only virtuous because it is associated with morally good actions. Of course, tending to produce morally good actions can be one good feature of virtuous attention, and it is compatible with it being virtuous in the way I've suggested: Ben's attention to where the shoes he is buying were manufactured is morally important not only because it helps him to avoid supporting unjust labor practices but also reflects well on his moral character by manifesting his morally important concern for justice. He is the kind of person who cares deeply about global justice, and his attention exhibits this concern. This attention both helps him to act well *and* shows that justice matters to him.

But virtuous attention can also reflect well on one's character without issuing in overt behavior. Imagine a young boy from a well-off family whose very large house has a staff of mostly Hispanic workers. The boy is not particularly close with them, but he cares about them as equals and so can't help but notice every time his father treats them with contempt. Suppose that because of his position in the family and his father's stubbornness, he is not in a position to do anything about the situation. Despite his lack of action, his attention shows moral concern and reflects well on him—he is a *better* person than his brother, who does not care at all about the workers, and so takes their father's poor treatment of them for granted.

Attending to the news of a distant tragedy can reflect well on someone if such attention manifests a concern for those harmed. This can be true even if the witness is unable to do anything to change things (think of the importance some put on "bearing witness" to tragedy, even if unable to affect its course). Even if such attention is not useful for bringing about good effects, it can still reflect well on the moral character of those who bear witness. Again, this is only if the attention manifests genuine concern for those affected, not if it manifests morbid curiosity or ill will.

This type of attention is open to creatures like Weather Watchers or those with locked-in syndrome. A Weather Watcher who notices the rain falling on others is better than one who fails to notice out of a lack of concern for others. Someone with locked-in syndrome can notice the progress of a fellow patient because he cares about them or notice the kindness and dedication of a doctor. Though neither can express this attention, it reflects well on them all the same.

The same goes for cases of vicious attention. The bully (childhood or otherwise) noticing weakness in others because he cares about exerting power over them. The racist attending to the ethnicity of the name on an application because she cares about not having "one of them" working in her department. These are all ways in which malicious concerns manifest in conscious attention. These states can be bad because of their connection to morally wrong actions, but they can be vicious even if no such actions occur. If the bully never gets a chance to pick on the weak child because the teachers are too watchful or if the racist is not on the hiring committee, such attention still manifests morally bad concerns and so are vicious.

I began with a scene starring a friend who, in the middle of an important conversation with you, attends to their smartphone instead of what you are saying. I suggested that their attention reflects poorly on them both as a friend and as a conversational partner because it manifests a lack of concern for you and for the topic of conversation. It reflects poorly on them because it manifests something about what matters to them, about their priorities.

Of course, there is something bad about *expressing* a lack of concern in this situation; checking one's phone during an important conversation with a friend is bad *behavior*. But even if this friend did not express this lack of attention, it could still manifests a lack of concern for what you are saying. Suppose they left their phone in the car and so simply sit there *thinking* about what messages might have arrived in their inbox instead of listening to you. Their attention still manifests a lack of concern for what you are saying and, in this sense, reflects poorly on them even if it is not overtly expressed.

Reality, as usual, is more complex. If the friend is, say, reading celebrity gossip, then it does reflect poorly on them because it shows that they care more about gossip than what you're talking about or a basic level of respect for you. But suppose you learn that their mother is in the hospital for heart surgery and they're expecting word about her condition at any minute. Or suppose you learn that the friend has a severe case of undiagnosed ADD. These facts are relevant to how their attention reflects on them. Explaining virtuous and vicious attention by its connection with concern helps us to understand why—because in these cases, though their attention is the same, the cares and concerns that underlie it are very different.

SCRUPULOSITY: AN OBJECTION

If attention is virtuous when manifesting moral concern, what about constant or excessive attention to moral matters? Does this account make a virtue out of being morally neurotic? It does not, primarily because it is not the frequency or intensity of attention that determines how morally virtuous it is.

This can be seen clearly in cases of scrupulosity, a species of obsessive-compulsive disorder that involves persistent thoughts or urges about moral and religious matters and an inability to ignore or eliminate them. Scrupulosity has both behavioral and emotional dimensions, but it also involves certain patterns of conscious attention. Consider J. J. Keeler's description of how her scrupulosity affected her when driving:

> Idling at stop signs and traffic lights was the worst. I was sure a
> pedestrian would walk in front of my car the second I resumed
> driving. This led me to study the road carefully in front of me,

sometimes waiting at a stop sign for one or two minutes before I felt comfortable proceeding. Other times, I'd go through a traffic light and then pull over on the side of the road, turning my head back so I could study the ground I'd just driven over. I was always looking for a body. Checking didn't quiet all the doubts. Instead, I'd worry that whoever I hit had simply disappeared from my sight. They had crawled into a field, fallen behind a tree, rolled into the gutter. This caused me to check even more, peering down water drains and searching nearby parking lots, looking for the bruised and bloodied.[24]

Not only does scrupulosity involve certain behaviors, but also paying attention in certain ways. Over and over she attends to many things out of a concern to avoid injuring or killing a pedestrian. Though this example centers on a behavioral action, this need not be the case. She could attend over and over to whether or not she had a racist or envious thought. Since her attention manifests moral concern, is she more morally virtuous than the rest of us?

Part of the answer depends on to what extent her attention does manifest moral concern. It can be difficult to determine to what extent the attention associated with scrupulosity manifests a concern to avoiding harm or racist thoughts and to what extent it manifests a concern to reduce one's own anxiety and fulfill the urge to check.[25] It matters to how virtuous the associated attention is, whether scrupulosity is more like extreme moral contentiousness or more like scratching an itch.

24. Keeler (2012, 96).
25. Recently, Summers and Sinnott-Armstrong (forthcoming) offer a detailed discussion of many of the moral issues surrounding scrupulosity; they argue persuasively that scrupulosity is not virtuous on similar grounds. Thanks to Jesse Summers for helpful discussion of these issues.

If we assume that Keeler's attention does in fact manifest a morally important concern for the safety of others, that her attention is not a kind of experiential tic, then it is virtuous. What may still be tic-like, however, is being reminded of this concern over and over again. Even if her concerns are genuine, her obsessive-compulsive disorder acts like an annoying child with a one-track mind. Though her state of attention is connected to her cares, the frequency of being in such states does not. As with emotions, more frequent and intense attention does not always manifest a greater degree of concern. It is likely that most drivers care about the safety of pedestrians as much as Keeler; the only difference is they do not have a mental disorder constantly screaming it in their ear.

There can also be something less than virtuous about the kind of moral concerns associated with scrupulosity; they are often very narrow and focused exclusively on specific rules. Jennifer Traig, whose scrupulosity took a more religious form, describes Judaism as having "an embarrassment of riches for the compulsive practitioner" and goes on to explain:

> As a result, most scrupulous Jews tend to overlook, even violate, the bulk of the laws while observing one or two with excruciating care . . . .. I was happy to lie to my dishonored parents while breaking the Sabbath, as long as it was in the service of getting my hands ritually clean.[26]

This highlights an important difference between our overall evaluations of the virtuous person and the scrupulous person: We expect a devoted Jewish person to care about following *all* of the laws (or at least *most* of them!). We also expect a good person to care about a

26. Traig (2004, 35).

sufficiently wide range of moral goods. A good person cares about not harming others in all kinds of ways, only one of which is by running them over. Keeler's attention to her driving means she must pay less attention to other moral goods like meeting someone on time or the needs of those around her more generally.

We have limited reserves of conscious attention. Paying attention to this sentence means you are not at the same time paying attention to what is happening outside your window or how a close friend is feeling now. When one specific care, though morally good, takes up all one's attention, then other morally good concerns will be neglected. This is a tradeoff that will matter to the virtuous person.

ATTENTION AND GRATITUDE

Sometimes virtuous attention is not directed toward our own actions or mental states, but to external benefits. It is this kind of attention that is associated with gratitude. We think of virtuous people as noticing when others help them out; they consciously acknowledge the benefits they receive and attend to those that provided them. This conscious attention is a critical aspect of gratitude.[27]

Gratitude is, of course, a complex phenomenon. It has an affective aspect, which allows it to be virtuous in the same way as other emotions. It also involves conscious attention, which will be my focus here. The attention involved in gratitude is involuntary, though it is

---

27. It is more accurate, however, to describe it as a response to a *perceived* benefit; suppose I have a birthday party and a guest brings me gift box that, because of the markings, I assume is something I want very much so I feel grateful. Now suppose that upon opening the box, I discover that it is empty; there is only a sarcastic card, the result of a practical joke. I may *no longer* feel grateful, but it would be wrong to say that I *never* really felt gratitude at all. My gratitude may have been hasty and mistaken, but it was gratitude nonetheless.

often cultivated through voluntary action, and may go unexpressed in overt action. Understanding the attentive aspect of gratitude helps to explain many of its key features and why it is a moral virtue.

Gratitude is, most generally, an attitude toward a benefit that we receive and its source. We can distinguish thankfulness, an attitude about a benefit, from gratitude, a response aimed at those who provided the benefit. I may simply be thankful *for* having something to eat, but I am grateful *to* my friend for buying the meal.[28]

Gratitude is directed to a variety of different objects and often in complex ways. On the ground, not all gratitude is of the simple "I'm grateful to John for helping me move last week" kind. To see this, consider Daniel Dennett's reflections on how to direct his gratitude after surviving risky emergency heart surgery:

> To whom, then, do I owe my gratitude? To the cardiologist who has kept me alive and ticking for years, and who swiftly and confidently rejected the original diagnosis of nothing worse than pneumonia. To the surgeons, neurologists, anesthesiologists, and the perfusionist, who kept my systems going for many hours under daunting circumstances. To the dozen or so physician assistants, nurses, physical therapists, x-ray technicians, and a small army of phlebotomists so deft that you hardly know they are drawing your blood. The people who brought the meals, kept my room clean, did the mountains of laundry generated by such a messy case, wheeled

---

28. Walker (1980, 45ff.) makes a similar, but terminologically awkward distinction between "gratitude" (directed to someone) and "gratefulness" (more general thankfulness). Some, like Comte-Sponville (1996, 132ff.), take the appreciative aspect of gratitude to mean that it is always pleasurable. I will not rely on this in my account and I'm not sure it is true: Suppose it is important to me to make a journey on my own, without the help of others. If I run into a serious problem and someone helps me, I may feel grateful but find it displeasurable. Or imagine receiving a thoughtful gift from a romantic rival; you may feel grateful, but not find it particularly pleasurable.

me to x-ray, and so forth. These people came from Uganda, Kenya, Liberia, Haiti, the Philippines, Croatia, Russia, China, Korea, India—and the United States, of course—and I have never seen more impressive mutual respect, as they helped each other and checked each other's work. But for all their teamwork, this local gang could not have done their job without the huge background of contributions from others. I remember with gratitude my late friend and Tufts colleague, physicist Allan Cormack, who shared the Nobel Prize for his invention of the CT scanner. Allan—you have posthumously saved yet another life, but who's counting? The world is better for the work you did. Thank goodness. Then there is the whole system of medicine, both the science and the technology, without which the best-intentioned efforts of individuals would be roughly useless. So I am also grateful to the editorial boards and referees, past and present, of Science, Nature, Journal of the American Medical Association, Lancet, and all the other institutions of science and medicine that keep churning out improvements, detecting and correcting flaws.[29]

Dennett describes a mix of thankfulness and gratitude, but his gratitude admits of a variety of objects; it is directed not only at particular individuals, but also the systems and institutions that created the conditions for those individuals to function in harmony. He directs his gratitude toward a large number of persons and to the situational factors that allowed them to act as they did.

It's critical to distinguish gratitude as an inner response from the outward expressions and actions commonly associated with it. It is possible to experience gratitude without expressing it and to express it without experiencing it: A student can be grateful to her professor

29. Dennett (2007, 114).

for extending an impending deadline without ever expressing it, and a recent graduate can write thank-you cards until his hand cramps without feeling an ounce of gratitude at all.

Though gratitude is often associated with outward acts of recompense, it does not *require* them. One can be grateful to someone even though, for various social and personal reasons, expressing it outwardly may be inappropriate or harmful. Someone in a repressive regime may feel grateful to distant rebels or to a foreign leader who has spoken out for their cause but be unable to express such gratitude without endangering themselves or their family. We can also feel gratitude to those who have died long ago or to anonymous benefactors. Such gratitude can go unexpressed for lack of anyone to express it to. Of course, gratitude generally does involve various intentions and behaviors, but they are neither necessary nor sufficient for experiencing the inner attitude. A final thought of gratitude moments before one's death is genuine gratitude, even if it remains unexpressed.

Gratitude also paradigmatically involves conscious attention and, at least in some cases, requires it. Being grateful is, after all, often contrasted with "taking things for granted"—with paying insufficient attention to benefits one receives.[30] Of course, attention to benefits and their source is not sufficient for gratitude. A teenager under the influence of Nietzsche, for example, might attend to the benefits his parents have provided for him but take it to be evidence of how disgustingly weak Mom and Dad are.

Attention alone is insufficient for gratitude, but does gratitude *require* attention? When Emma avoids walking into a tree while intently thinking about a philosophical argument, she does not attend to the tree, though her awareness of it allows her to avoid

---

30. Walker (1980, 42) seems to take some kind of conscious recognition to be necessary for gratitude.

it. Something similar seems to be possible for gratitude; one can be aware of benefits and respond to them without attending to them. The idea of "subconscious gratitude" does not seem to be self-contradictory in the same way as "subconscious deliberation" or "subconscious reflection" can seem.[31] Someone who was a particularly unreflective teenager might discover, years later, that he subconsciously appreciated all that his single father did for him. "I didn't think about it at the time" we can imagine him reflecting, "but in hindsight I see that I felt grateful for everything he did for me." He might, for example, come to see many previously mysterious actions, things like washing his father's car without being asked, as expressions of this subconscious gratitude. Though it isn't paradigmatic, it is at least *possible* to experience gratitude on a visceral level, without consciously recognizing it or reflecting upon it.

Even if the very notion of being grateful does not require conscious reflection, in many cases both gratitude and thankfulness require conscious attention for psychological reasons. Many benefits are so complex and subtle that we cannot respond to them without conscious, reflective thought. This is often true of situational benefits: Think about how difficult it often is to get many people to see the subtle institutional benefits they enjoy. In a famous essay, Peggy McIntosh describes how she often encountered men who were willing to accept that women were often disadvantaged but still denied that they experienced any advantages because of their gender.

In dealing with these issues, she found that she herself had taken for granted many advantages of being white in America. She lists many privileges that are subtle and difficult for a white person to

---

31. For example, see Korsgaard (1996, 100) on the link between deliberation and conscious reflection.

see without conscious reflection. She names many such benefits like being able to see a film with people of one's own race represented, not being asked to speak for all members of one's race, and being able to choose where to live without thinking of the risk of racial violence, to name just a few on her list. She describes such benefits as making up an "invisible knapsack"—invisible because the benefits are so difficult to see. Her description of her own response to these benefits provides evidence of their subtlety. She writes, "I repeatedly forgot each of the realizations on this list until I wrote it down."[32] Even for smart, thoughtful people, recognizing some benefits will require conscious reflection on history, the nature of justice, and the very structure of institutions.

Many of the benefits we enjoy are difficult, if not impossible, to appreciate without conscious reflection. One may be unable to appreciate the benefit of citizenship in a country with a free press, for example, without reflection on the nature of government, what the press is, and how it works. Recall that after being in the hospital, Daniel Dennett was grateful to peer-reviewed medical journals and those who keep them running. This kind of gratitude is impossible without some knowledge of how journals work, what editorial boards do, and how medical science advances—complex knowledge that requires conscious attention. These factors contribute to a successful surgery, but do so in ways that are diffuse and difficult for us to see without conscious reflection. It is not the sort of benefit most of us can feel viscerally or subconsciously, at least not right away. It requires conscious reflection because the subtlety and complexity of the benefits and the systems that produce them make them especially difficult to see.

---

32. McIntosh (1988, 190). Though she initially needed to act in order to *cultivate* the relevant attention, after she has done this, her conscious attention may be involuntary.

Conscious attention in particular plays an important role in the way in which gratitude is virtuous. Conscious attention can manifest cares and concerns, and when those cares are morally important the attention is virtuous. Many moral goods, particularly subtle and complex ones, require conscious reflection in order to respond with gratitude. Such attention, though conscious, need not be expressed as overt action. It can even be involuntary: After a few weeks of deliberately attending to the complex benefits you've received, you can find yourself spontaneously reflecting on such things when visiting a hospital or being treated respectfully by a police officer.

The cares and concerns that underlie the attention involved in gratitude explain why gratitude is virtuous and ingratitude is vicious: Ingratitude is vicious because it manifests a lack of concern for sources of value outside ourselves. It is part of a family of vicious states that stem from excessive self-concern; after all, a central issue of morality is managing self-concern and other-concern.

Gratitude is virtuous because it shows that one cares about the external sources of one's own benefits. We are not grateful to our own hard work; we are grateful to others who helped us along. Concern for the benefits we receive and their source manifests an appreciation of the sacrifices of others that is morally good.

This is why in many cases being grateful is more virtuous than merely being thankful. The thankful person is glad to have been helped; they care primarily about the benefit. The grateful person, however, also appreciates the helper; they care about the *source* of the benefit too. The attentive aspect of gratitude is relevant when distinguishing it from merely being thankful. Gratitude is directed at the source of a benefit, while being thankful simply involves being glad that one received a benefit. Being thankful rather than grateful is not *always* less virtuous: It is not less virtuous if I am merely thankful that my plants were watered while I was on vacation because I didn't know that a friend came over to water them and simply thought it rained while I was away.

However, to simply feel thankful that an important group project was finished when I know that Jason stayed up all night to finish it *is* less virtuous. This is because being thankful rather than grateful manifests a lack of concern for Jason's contribution. It shows a lack of concern for the efforts, hardships, and good will of others if a father is merely thankful that his son was saved when he knows that a team of firefighters risked their lives to save him. Here the lack of attention to the source of a benefit reflects poorly on someone because it manifests a lack of concern.

Understanding gratitude as manifesting concern helps to explain when misdirected gratitude is vicious and when it is not. Sometimes misdirected gratitude manifests concern and sometimes it does not. If I ask my mother who picked her up at the airport and I mishear "Tom picked me up" as "Don picked up me" and I feel grateful to Don, my gratitude is misdirected. It does not, however, manifest anything about my concerns. My misdirected gratitude is, we might say, "an honest mistake".

But not all misdirected gratitude is the result of an honest mistake. Someone who never directs their gratitude to people of a certain race or sex manifests racist or sexist attitude in their gratitude. Once after several days of waiting for a visa at an Indian embassy, the woman in the next line realized that she did not have the proper currency to pay her fee. My friend gave her the money, so she would not have to wait in line for another day in the hot sun. Immediately after receiving the money from my friend, she turned her back and expressed thanks that *the gods* had helped her this day. Even in the context of a religious worldview, it manifests a lack of concern for the hardship and goodwill of my friend to direct gratitude *only* toward the gods (it is, after all, *my friend* who now had less money!).

BUDDHIST GRATITUDE

Buddhist thought discusses a wide variety of gratitude. Many forms are similar to the types discussed earlier: gratitude to parents, teachers, and friends for the benefits they provide us. There is also a more exceptional form of gratitude that many Buddhist thinkers advocate: gratitude toward those that intend to harm us.

Many in the West would object that this cannot really be gratitude because gratitude is, by definition, directed toward those who intend to *benefit* us.[33] This condition seems too narrow; recall that even when Dennett's gratitude was directed toward persons, many of these people did not have the intention to benefit *him* in particular, and may not have had an intention of benefitting anyone at all. Even if the inventors of the CT scanner or the editorial boards of various medical journals simply aimed at improving their résumés, Dennett can still feel gratitude for their role in saving his life.

Buddhist gratitude extends beyond those that merely did not intend to benefit us to also include those that intend to *harm* us. Whether or not this response is, strictly speaking, rightly called "gratitude," it has much in common with it.[34] It is an inner response to a benefit, though one of a special type, and its source. It is a high-level virtue, possessed by those working toward an ethical ideal of selfless compassion for all beings. Most importantly for my purposes here, it is an inner state with a strong attentive component.

---

33. See Heider (1958), Berger (1975), Simmons (1979, 171-2), and McConnell (1993, 44) who take gratitude to be directed only toward those that intended to benefit us. Strawson (1962, 76) merely makes this a condition of *rational* gratitude. Since I have argued that irrational states can still be virtuous, I can accept that such gratitude may be irrational, though I will not take a stand either way.
34. See Fitzgerald (1998, 123ff.) for a defense of this response as gratitude.

Having this kind of Buddhist gratitude (or, if you'd prefer, *gratitude-like* response) toward those who harm us is explicitly advocated in many Tibetan Buddhist texts. To pick one famous example, Gyalsé Thogmé highlights it in his description of a *bodhisattva*, a spiritual and ethical ideal in Buddhism:

> While in the midst of a large group,
> If someone insults you and reveals your flaws,
> See them as a spiritual friend.
> To respectfully bow to them
> is the practice of *bodhisattvas*.[35]

This advice was also given earlier by Langri Tangpa, another Tibetan thinker:

> Even if you are harmed by someone
> Whom you have helped
> And have great hopes for,
> See them as a true spiritual guide.[36]

It is not hard to notice when someone is mistreating you or pointing out your faults in public. What *is* difficult is to notice that such situations are opportunities to practice virtue.[37] One must be careful

---

35. This is verse fifteen of *The Thirty-Seven Practices of Bodhisattvas* (Tibetan: *rgyal-sras lag-len so-bdun-ma*). The translation is my own.

36. This is verse six of his *Eight Verses for Training the Mind* (Tibetan: *blo sbyong tshigs brgyad ma*). Again, the translation is mine. This advice draws from similar instructions in Śāntideva (*BCA* VI.107 and 111).

37. The practice of seeing a harmer as an opportunity for practicing virtue is by no means unique to Buddhism. For example, in his *Meditations*, Marcus Aurelius offers similar advice: "When another's fault offends you, turn to yourself and consider what similar shortcomings are found in you. Do you, too, find your good in riches, pleasure, reputation, or such like?" (X.30).

here. Taken in isolation, this advice might be toxic by reinforcing patterns of abuse and victim blaming. It is important to remember that these instructions are directed specifically to Buddhist practitioners who have taken a vow to overcome self-attachment and eliminate the suffering of others.

Of course, the mere fact that one is thankful to be confronted with an aggressive person is not enough to make it virtuous; one might, for example, be grateful to those who insult because it provides an excuse to be violent in response or to indulge in feelings of resentment. The virtuous response requires an aim to respond to such difficulties with kindness and compassion.

And yet this type of Buddhist gratitude is not merely thankfulness for an opportunity to practice virtue. The response is primarily directed toward the person who provides the opportunity, the person who intends to harm us. So we are advised to respond to this person in ways that strongly resemble gratitude: by bowing to them and responding with compassion, care, and respect. Gyalsé Thogmé highlights this in other verses, instructing us to cherish those who betray us as a mother would her sick child or to see those who disparage us as spiritual teachers. We are to think of them as friends and guides; we are to hope they do well, and direct thanking language and gestures toward them.

In order for gratitude toward those that harm us to be virtuous, it must manifest morally good concern. The Buddhist case does just that: Gratitude toward those who intend to harm us manifests a concern to care for others, even under the most difficult circumstances, even when they exhibit ill will toward us. It manifests a concern to respond with compassion even when it is unbelievably hard. These underlying concerns are made clear in the practice: One is not, for example, advised to go around hurting others to give them a chance to practice responding in this way.

Along with affective aspects, this response involves attending to the other person in a certain way. In involves seeing them as a teacher or friend and reflecting on their difficulties and desire to be happy. Someone with this response has an aim to treat *all* beings with compassion and kindness, so a person who tries to harm or create difficulties gives a special kind of benefit: the chance to have compassion toward those who do not wish us well. As Buddhist teachers often put it, this person gives us a benefit that no Buddha ever could. Again, we're not merely glad that the situation happened, but we see the other person as a teacher and wish them well. Such attention, then, is morally virtuous by manifesting various morally important concerns: the concern to feel compassion for *all* beings, even those who bear us ill will, and the concern to respond to malicious people with kindness.

This responsiveness, of course, need not be behavioral—maintaining or testing one's compassion may be an internal matter, such as emotionally enduring a difficult situation. One may, in the course of practice, avoid certain behaviors or seek out certain situations, but these are ways of *cultivating* the response; they are not the same as inner gratitude. A Weather Watcher may be thankful for the arrival of the monsoon, seeing it as an opportunity develop greater patience in the face of bad weather. We can imagine a Buddhist Weather Watcher feeling gratitude toward a malicious gardener who knowingly sprays water on them, internally feeling compassion and thanking the gardener as their spiritual teacher. Such responses are also open to someone with locked-in syndrome who cultivates a spontaneous gratitude toward a particularly rude hospital worker without any overt actions at all.

Aside from the extreme Buddhist version, gratitude of all types involves paying attention to benefits and their sources. This response is virtuous by manifesting morally important cares and concerns.

Sometimes it is a concern for others and what they have done for us, while in more extreme cases it can be a concern to thank those for the chance to respond compassionately, even in the most difficult of circumstances. This attention is often involuntary, though it may be cultivated via voluntary actions, and often remains within, unexpressed in overt action.

ATTENTION AND MODESTY

It is not only attention that can be virtuous or vicious but also inattention. Just as we think of a virtuous person as noticing benefits and their sources, there are also things we expect them *not* to pay much attention to. Virtuous people aren't constantly sizing others up and don't spend much of their time dwelling on how virtuous they are. This is the heart of the virtue of modesty. Modesty in this sense has little to do with revealing clothing or one's sex life; it is about the relationship we have to our own goodness and how this manifests as attention and *in*attention.[38]

Modesty is a dependent virtue; being modest requires some other good quality for us to be modest *about*.[39] Someone is modest about their cooking ability, generosity, or physical strength. It can be tempting to think that modesty is always about *one's own* good qualities. This need not be the case, however. Modesty is often about good qualities not of one's *own*, but only related to oneself in some way. A mother can be immodest when she boasts about her son's grades. A Detroiter can be immodest when talking about the performance of the Red Wings. A modern Greek can be immodest

---

38. I give a more detailed defense of modesty as a virtue of attention in Bommarito (2013).
39. See Slote (1983, 61).

when bragging about the intellectual achievements of Socrates, Plato, and Aristotle. If the people in cases like these are in fact behaving immodestly, it seems that the quality one is modest about need not be one's own, but simply closely related to oneself (*my* child, *my* team, *my* people).[40]

Modesty has two notable features.[41] One is the possibility of false modesty. Some people are not modest but are simply playing the part. These people may be *acting* modestly; they might say the right words and assume the right postures, but they're faking it. The existence of these fakers rules out accounts of modesty that reduce it to a set of overt behaviors. Modesty cannot be just acting in a certain way, because there are people who *do* act that way but are not modest.

The second notable feature is that modesty is difficult to self-attribute. There is something self-defeating about saying the sentence, "I am modest"—saying it is an *im*modest thing to do! This suggests something about the trait; if you've got it, you won't know it (and if you *seem* to know about it, then you must not really have it).[42]

Understanding modesty as rooted in attention best explains both of these features: A commonsense way to understand what it is to be modest about something is to not make a big deal about it, downplay it, or ignore it. We ignore things by directing our attention *away* from them. In this sense, modesty is often a virtue of *in*attention. We can be modest through inattention in two ways: quality inattention and value inattention.

---

40. Because there is no natural way to talk about the good qualities closely related to oneself, I will often refer to the relation modest people have to their own good qualities. Talk of "one's own good qualities" in my discussion should be understood in this wider sense, referring to any good quality related to oneself.
41. These features are taken from Driver (2001, 17ff.).
42. See Sorensen (1988, 160) and Driver (1989, 2001).

A person can be modest about a quality simply by directing their attention away from the quality itself. They can be modest by ignoring good qualities that are closely related to them. Consider Kelly, who has several good qualities we have discussed so far; she cares deeply about others and so often experiences *mudita*, gratitude, and sympathy. Kelly doesn't think much about these things, though; she doesn't care much about patting herself on the back, so she doesn't spend much time reflecting on her own good qualities. She has this kind of conscious mental life not out of deliberate effort, but as a natural manifestation of what matters most to her.[43]

Another way to put it is that Kelly avoids what Bernard Williams called moral self-indulgence: Those who are morally self-indulgent care disproportionately about their own morality; as Williams put it, "what the agent cares about is not so much other people, as *himself* caring about other people."[44] A person who dwells on how patient or generous *they* are betrays a self-centered kind of moral concern; they are more concerned with their own virtue than with other people. Caring about morality in this self-centered way can be a sign of not being morally concerned enough; a truly virtuous person would be most concerned with the well-being of those to which they are patient or generous.

Moral self-indulgence explains why immodesty often takes a comparative form: Someone who is immodest often focuses not only on their own good qualities in isolation but on comparative judgments. They attend to ways in which they are *better* or *more virtuous* than others. Again, this manifests concerns that seem at odds

---

43. Similar strands can be found lurking in other accounts of modesty: Ridge (2000, 277) suggests that modest people "de-emphasize" what they are modest about, and Raterman (2006, 228) describes the modest as "reluctant" to evaluate themselves in terms of their goodness. An important way to de-emphasize or downplay something is to ignore it.
44. Williams (1981, 45ff.).

with what matters to a good person. A good person's mental life doesn't center on constantly sizing up others; they will, of course, care about being generous, but because they're not morally self-indulgent, they won't care much about being *more generous* than others.

Sometimes, however, a modest person *does* pay attention to their own good qualities. Such a person is not modest through inattention, but by directing toward attention *toward* the external sources of such qualities. Suppose David has the same good qualities as Kelly but also often directs his attention to them. When he does so, however, David considers how fortunate he has been: He attends to his qualities while reflecting on how he wouldn't have them without a stable upbringing, caring friends and family, and a host of other factors. This is characteristic of David's attention; he attends to his own good qualities but in a way that manifests concern for the help and good fortune that brought them about.

David seems modest not because of what he ignores, but because of what he *does not* ignore. Even though he attends to his good qualities and their value, he also attends to the role of forces of circumstance and luck in producing those qualities. This intuition is what leads many to claim that the modest person keeps perspective: An essential part of keeping perspective is attending to the external conditions that allowed for the quality one is modest about.[45]

As before, attention alone is not sufficient: An arrogant person can attend to circumstance when belittling its role, but one cannot keep perspective without it. Attending in these ways is not sufficient for modesty; it must happen for the right reasons. Those who are inattentive to their good qualities only because an attention disorder prevents them from attending to anything for very long or because

45. See Flanagan (1990), Nuyen (1998), and Raterman (2006).

they are the kind of pessimists who never attend to any good qualities at all are not modest. When we take Kelly or David to be modest, we take their patterns of attention to manifest their cares and concerns. David counts as modest because his frequent attention to external factors in his success is a manifestation of his concern for the role of such factors.

Inattentive modesty like Kelly's can also manifest concern; it can be the result of a *lack* of certain cares or concerns. Her inattention to her own good qualities is not an instance of modesty if it is the result of untreated ADD or a pessimistic temperament. However, when it manifests a lack of bad concerns, like the concern to ogle her own self-image, Kelly's inattention is modest; it manifests a lack of certain self-centered concerns.

Like being a grateful person, being modest involves a pattern of attention over time. In the case of modesty, this pattern is characterized by an *inattentiveness* to one's own good qualities, the value of such qualities, and one's own role in bringing them about. This inattentiveness manifests a lack of self-centered concerns and a concern for the help given by others. It does not require *complete* lack of attention to one's own good qualities; isolated instances of attention will not spoil one's modesty. It does, however, require that one not dwell on these things.[46]

Of course, the line between mere occasional noticing and dwelling is fuzzy, and it can be difficult to tell how much attention is too much. This vagueness does not mean that the distinction between dwelling and mere attending cannot play any explanatory role. There are definite cases of dwelling, as when someone spends

---

46. This is similar to Hastings Rashdall's take on modesty: "we should disapprove of any habitual dwelling with satisfaction upon one's own capacities or one's own merits" (1907, 205). Thanks to Thomas Hurka for this reference.

night and day thinking about a mean remark or about a loved one. There are also definite cases of noticing without dwelling, as when we notice the dirty dishes in the sink but do not give them a second thought.

The role of attention in modesty explains both the existence of false modesty and the problems with self-attribution. Since attention is not merely acting in a certain way, but an internal feature of our mental lives, it explains false modesty. Consider the difference between paying attention to a story your friend is telling you and *acting* as if you are paying attention. To be modest, David cannot simply act as if he is paying attention to the role fortune played in his success; he must *really* pay attention to it.

The same is true of inattention. There is a difference between ignoring someone at a party and acting as if you are ignoring them. You might be acting as if you are ignoring a former friend by not looking in their direction and not reacting to things they say, but internally your attention may be totally focused on the friend you are *pretending* to ignore. The same is true of modesty; those who only pretend to ignore certain good qualities are guilty of false modesty.

As with other inner states, creatures such as Weather Watchers or people with full-body paralysis can have the patterns of attention I've described, even though they cannot perform overt actions or form intentions. Stone Weather Watchers can be modest about their own keen eyesight, patience, or any other good qualities. Someone with locked-in syndrome can dwell on the dedication and skill of his doctor rather than on his own courage. Their lack of self-centeredness can manifest as patterns of attention just like those of Kelly or David.

Explaining modesty in terms of attention also explains why uttering the sentence "I am modest" seems self-defeating. Uttering such a sentence, however, is not *always* self-defeating.[47] Consider Steven, who actually is quite modest. One day when out with friends, Steven's modest nature becomes the topic of conversation. Naturally, Steven is not interested in discussing the issue and denies that he has any outstanding virtue. But the more he denies it, the more adamant his friends become that he *really* is one of the most modest people they know. They cite incident after incident to illustrate his modesty. Finally, Steven reluctantly admits, "All right, all right—I'm modest. Can we please talk about something else?" In this context, Steven's utterance of "I'm modest" does not seem to detract from his modesty, but rather is an expression of it.

An attention-based account explains both why self-attributing modesty is self-undermining in general, and why Steven's utterance does not undermine his modesty. In most contexts, saying "I am modest" involves directing attention toward a good quality, modesty itself. However, when Steven says it, he is directing attention *away* from his good quality; he reluctantly admits it so everyone can move on to the next topic of conversation.

Insofar as modesty is a good quality, modesty entails metamodesty. If Kelly dwells on her own inattention to her good qualities, she is not being modest because she *is* dwelling on one of her good qualities—her modesty. It is not clear that one can attend to one's inattention to an object without also attending to the object. Thinking about how you never think about ice cream *is* thinking about ice cream. Similarly, dwelling on how you never dwell on how great you are *is* dwelling on how great you are.

Things get more complex for those, like David, who are modest by attending to the role external factors play in creating and

---

47. Raterman (2006, 232) makes a similar point; his example is of uttering the sentence in the context of a quiet conversation with a good friend.

sustaining his good qualities. David might pay attention to how much he attends to external factors when considering his good qualities. But if he is modest *about his modesty*, he will also consider the role of external factors in directing his attention in this way. It does not seem to spoil his modesty if David also reflects, "I guess I am pretty modest, but it's all thanks to how my parents raised me and how many supportive friends I have that I am able to be so." Here David manages to be modest about his own modesty by focusing on the role of situational factors in bringing it about. Of course, this reflection need not be expressed to count as virtuous; it reflects well on him even if it is completely private and unexpressed.

What, then, is so bad about dwelling on your own good qualities, their importance, or your own role in bringing them about? An immodest person wears a kind of mental blinders, which push aside many things of value. It is a feature of conscious attention that in attending to something one ignores another: While you are attending to this sentence, you are not attending to the weather outside your window or what time it is. Immodest people, by overattending to their own goodness, do so at the expense of attending to good qualities in others, which can stand in the way of meaningful relationships. By constantly focusing on their own good qualities, the immodest person experiences the world through a self-centered lens, which is a bad way to experience life. Attending to the good qualities of others allows for the valuable and positive experience of sympathetic joy at the successes of others. It also allows one to recognize capable teachers and opportunities to learn from others.

This is not to say that appreciating your good qualities or even noticing them once in a while is vicious. In one sense, "inattention" to something means that one completely ignores it; to say that I did not bring an umbrella because of my inattention to the weather means I didn't notice the clouds at all. However, in another sense, "inattention" means that one pays little attention to something; to say that a husband is inattentive to his wife does not require that he *never* directs his attention toward his wife, only that he does so infrequently. It is inattention in the latter sense that is related to modesty. A single swallow does not a summer make—it is not as if a single moment of attention to her own good qualities would spoil Kelly's modesty.

When we talk of virtues in general, we make assumptions about human psychology in general. Modesty is a virtue because, in general, people have a tendency to dwell on their own successes and to overlook the role of external conditions in bringing them about. For most of us, it is easy to notice our own name when provided a list of grant recipients or for our gaze to linger on our own face when shown a group photo. Or recall Bertrand Russell's emotive conjugations: I am firm; you are obstinate; he is a pig-headed fool.

This tendency, however, is far from universal. There are people who find it difficult to notice their own good qualities and have trouble extending their natural charity and appreciation for others to themselves. People like this may need to devote more of their attention to their own good qualities. Someone who has a tendency to dwell on their failures and bad qualities might do well to attend to their good qualities more than someone who finds it all too easy to dwell on their own success. If Kermit the Frog is miserable because he has a hard time noticing the good qualities he has, then it is good for him to sing a song every day that draws his attention to the good things about being green. The virtues need not be a one-size-fits-all affair, and modesty is no exception. But given general human tendencies, modesty is still a virtue for most of us.

Modesty involves patterns of attention that manifest morally important concerns. It manifests care for sources of value outside of oneself and a lack of selfish and vain concerns. This attention is often involuntary and need not be expressed in overt action—it is a way in which one's conscious mental life manifests moral concern. Weather Watchers and those with locked-in sydrome can manifest this pattern of attention without any overt action at all. It is a feature of a good person that can be invisible from the outside.

CONCLUSION

Simone Weil, one of the few champions of the moral importance of attention, reimagined the concept as a nuanced and technical one. Though she made use of a far more morally and spiritually loaded version of attention, she saw an important truth about the moral importance of our conscious mental lives. This comes out in a letter responding to someone who had read some of her writing:

> I was very moved to see that you had paid real attention to some pages I had shown you . . .. Attention is the rarest and purest form of generosity. It is given to very few minds to notice that things and beings exist. Since my childhood I have not wanted anything else but to receive the complete revelation of this before dying.[48]

So far, I've pushed against this: "I pay very close attention to people," the psychopath can reply, "when I am cutting someone, I attend to nothing but the person in front of me. I am deeply engrossed in every whimper and every quiver." Racists and snipers both attend to others, but their attention is not very rare and not very much like generosity at all.

48. Quoted in Pétrement (1976/1988, 462).

What Weil is praising is the sort of attention rooted in a fundamental concern for another person; attention that manifests an underlying care for someone else. There are times when we acknowledge someone's humanity, what a Kantian might call dignity, by giving to them our full conscious attention.[49] Simone Weil rightly saw that it is in these all too rare moments of attention that we manifest a deep concern for others.

Like generosity, this attention can be a natural manifestation of moral concern. Being present with them and attentive to them is a way of caring about them—about their well-being and about their value. Like generosity, some of us have to take voluntary steps to cultivate such a natural response and to overcome the many psychological, material, and situational factors that can get in the way.

Unlike generosity, this attention need not issue in overt action. One can acknowledge someone in this way without the person ever knowing about it. Simone Weil's correspondent paid real attention to her words even if they never wrote to her about it. When you care about someone, you think about them even when they are far away. You think about them after they have died. This conscious, attentive thought manifests your care even if they can never know about it, even when there is no outer sign of it at all. In the same way, a good person's cares and concerns manifest, in part, as a certain kind of conscious mental life. It is part of what makes them good, even though it is often invisible to the outside world.

---

49. Stephen Darwall (2006) describes how an eye condition (strabismus) led many to fail to notice when he was addressing them which gave him insights about how reciprocal recognition is central to morality.

Chapter 6

The Relevance of Inner Virtue

Our pleasures, emotions, and attention are all relevant to our moral character. They make a difference to what kind of people we are, even when confined to our inner lives and even when arising involuntarily. To evaluate someone is not simply to consider what they *do*, outwardly, in our shared social world. We are agents, but there is much more to us than that. This simple idea has relevance for both moral theory and practice.

MORAL THEORY

It is all too easy to define the subject of morality in a way that assumes it has a purely social and behavioral nature—morality as what we should and shouldn't *do* to each other, as how we should *behave* socially, publicly. Thinking of morality in this way can lead to a conception of the virtuous person simply as someone who behaves morally in a reliable enough way. This, in turn, makes it tempting to think that if we had the correct theory of moral action, we could easily derive an account of what a virtuous person is: someone who does those actions regularly.

To see morality in this way misses much of moral life, much of both the best and worst in people. The states I've focused on highlight some of the aspects of moral character that can remain disconnected from overt action: pleasures and emotions that remain within yet make a difference to what kind of person one is, the ways in which our conscious mental lives can manifest our deepest values and concerns. Evaluating a person is a distinct and complex kind of moral evaluation, not reducible to tendencies or collections of overt actions.

I've defended a theory of why such states are relevant to moral character, via a connection to underlying moral care and concern. This approach runs contrary to a variety of strands in virtue theory: The task of understanding what it means to be a good person need not involve producing a list of *the* virtues. This is a far more illuminating way to approach the question of what makes a good person. By thinking about what the core of being a good person is we can come to see what explains the various lists of traits we think of as virtuous or vicious.

There is a way in which, on my account, there is a single virtue—moral care. If a virtue must be unconditionally good, that is correct. The only unconditionally morally good trait one can have is to care about moral goods; this care, as Kant said about the good will, shines like a jewel on its own. Other states, and more broadly traits, are virtuous by realizing this care in a particular domain. A good person's inner states and outer actions, when virtuous, will manifest this concern.

This allows for cultural and personal diversity between virtuous people and, at the same time, explains what they have in common. If all I know about someone is that they are morally virtuous, how much do I know about them? The answer, I think, is not very much. I do not, for example, know if they have a cognitive or bodily impairment. I do not know much about their personality, temperament, and cultural outlook. I do not know how rational they are. I know that they care about moral goods like rights and well-being, but I do not know how such cares manifest through the lenses of their culture and individual personality. Injustice may make them sad, angry, both, or neither. Virtuous people are not clones of one another. They will have different personalities and cultural outlooks. What they share as virtuous people is a deep concern for moral goods.

For simplicity, I have talked about the "good person" or the "virtuous person." This, however, misleadingly suggests distinct classes of people with rigid boundaries—the virtuous, the vicious, and the rest of us. Reality, as usual, is much more complicated. Care, like the goodness or badness of people, comes in degrees. Deeper and stronger concern about moral goods makes one a morally better person. There need not be a rigid divide separating distinct moral classes of people.

In reality, there need not be ideally virtuous people in the world at all, or even very many minimally virtuous people. The kind of moral exemplars I've appealed to may be more a projection of our moral hopes and ambitions than a reflection of reality. At best, such exemplars are few and far between. Morally speaking, we're all dim matches that flicker in a very dark world. This makes it important to remember that the world contains light that's difficult, and sometimes even impossible, to see.

MORAL PRACTICE

If, as I've argued, involuntary mental states can be vicious, one might wonder: "If they're really involuntary, who cares? It's not like I can *do* anything about it." There are a few things to be said about this worry. Guidance is, to be sure, an important part of morality, but it is not the only part. We use moral standards not only to advise and guide action but also to evaluate. Remember that being vicious is not the same as being *blameworthy*. Someone may not be responsible or blameworthy for racist, sexist, or other malicious thoughts and feelings, but they're still a worse person than they would be without such states.

Such evaluations are also not as impractical as they may seem at first blush. Though we cannot voluntarily will our emotions, we can cultivate and discourage them. In this sense, our inner lives are a bit like a garden. To produce a beautiful garden, one must start with the seeds and soil at hand and contend with the oft-fickle weather. We take steps to encourage the plants to flourish, but they grow on their own, independently of our direct commands. A flourishing garden is a good thing, but it is not something we can simply will into being. And it is not something we are completely responsible for. This does not, however, mean that one has no effect on the beauty of one's garden, and it does not mean that there is nothing to be done to improve things.

Perhaps more importantly, reflecting on inner virtue and vice should make us more careful in our moral assessments of people. When we make moral assessments of others, we do so on the basis of limited evidence, and keeping in mind that there can be genuinely virtuous or vicious states that are invisible from the outside should make us even more modest about our confidence in such judgments.

This is a difficult lesson to learn. Once when teaching a class, I noticed a student constantly passing notes to the person next to her. Over the course of a few classes, as I saw her constantly passing notes, I thought to myself, "Well, she is clearly more interested in socializing with her friends than paying attention in class. Looks like she doesn't care much about learning philosophy or doing well in the class." I later learned that this student was very interested in philosophy, but because she was physically unable to speak, she would write down her questions and give them to the student next to her to ask out loud. I felt terrible.

Many of my philosopher friends attempted to console me by pointing out that my judgment was *rational*—it responded appropriately to the available evidence. Of course, we constantly have to make judgments about the inner lives of others based on just this kind of evidence. But if we keep in mind that there are inner states that are hard, if not impossible, to see from the outside, we will be more realistic about what we are doing and less confident in our evaluations of others.

The Chinese philosopher Liezi tells a story of a man who woke up one day to find his axe missing. When the man saw his neighbor's son, he noticed that the young man dressed like a thief, walked like a thief, and talked like a thief. The man later found his axe in the garden and subsequently noticed that the young man dressed, walked, and talked like an honest, upstanding young man.[1] We often project what we want to see onto other people, not realizing how very little we know about their inner lives.

It's easy to be fooled by outward appearances into thinking we know what is going on in another's head or heart, especially when making judgments about their character. We think there is no way that an elderly, soft-spoken woman could feel racial contempt. We think that someone with an accent, shaved head, and saffron robe doesn't care about money or sexual pleasure. Realizing that there are inner virtues and vices makes us far more sensitive to the fact that much of what is relevant to whether or not someone is a good person is concealed from our view.

1. This example is also found in the earlier *Spring and Autumn Annals* (*Lüshi Chunqiu*).

And yet such things *are* relevant to moral character. If we imagine evaluating people from God's point of view, we would look not only at what they've done but also at their inner lives. Most fundamentally, I think, we would want to know if their hearts were in the right place—if they cared about the right things. When sizing someone up, what matters most is what matters to them. And, for better or worse, that is often the kind of thing that is concealed within.

REFERENCES

Adams, Robert M. 2006. *A Theory of Virtue*. Oxford: Clarendon Press.

———. 1985. "Involuntary Sins." *The Philosophical Review* 94 (1): 3–31.

Allport, D. A. 1987. "Selection for Action." In *Perspectives on Perception and Action*, edited by H. Heuer and H. F. Sanders, 395–419. Mahwah, NJ: Lawrence Erlbaum Associates.

American Psychiatric Association. 2000. *Diagnostic and Statistical Manual of Mental Disorders* (4th ed.). Washington, DC: Author.

Annas, Julia. 2011. *Intelligent Virtue*. New York: Oxford University Press.

Anscombe, G. E. M. 1958/1997. "Modern Moral Philosophy." In *Virtue Ethics*, edited by Roger Crisp and Michael Slote, 26–44. New York: Oxford University Press.

Aquinas, Thomas. 1275/1948. *Summa Theologica*. Translated by Fathers of the Dominican Province. Notre Dame: Christian Classics.

Aristotle. 1999. Translated by Terence Irwin. *Nicomachean Ethics*. Indianapolis: Hackett.

Arpaly, Nomy. 2004. *Unprincipled Virtue*. Oxford: Oxford University Press.

———. 1999. "Hamlet and the Utilitarians." *Philosophical Studies* 99 (1): 46–57.

Arpaly, Nomy, and Timothy Schroeder. 2014. In *Praise of Desire*. Oxford: Oxford University Press.

Aurelius, Marcus. 2004. *Meditations*. Translated by Maxwell Staniforth. New York: Penguin Books.

Baier, Annette. 2010. *Reflections on How We Live*. New York: Oxford University Press.

———. 2008. *Death and Character*. Cambridge, MA: Harvard University Press.

Baker, Judith 1987. "Trust and Rationality." *Pacific Philosophical Quarterly* 68 (1): 1–13.

Baron, James. 2007. *Thinking and Deciding*. Cambridge: Cambridge University Press.

Bauby, Jean-Dominique. 1997/2007. *The Diving-Bell and the Butterfly*. Translated by Jeremy Leggatt. New York: Harper Perennial.

Bauer, Gerhard, Franz Gerstenbrand, and Erik Rumpl. 1979. "Varieties of the Locked-In Syndrome." *Journal of Neurology* 221 (2): 77–91.

Ben-Ze'ev, Aaron. 2000. *The Subtlety of Emotions*. Cambridge, MA: The MIT Press.

Berger, Fred R. 1975. "Gratitude." *Ethics* 85(4): 298–309.

Bharata. 2010. *The Nāṭyaśāstra*. Translated by Adya Rangacharya. New Delhi: Munshiram Manoharlal.

Bilimoria, Purushottama. 1995. "Ethics of Emotion: Some Indian Reflections." In *Emotions in Asian Thought*, edited by Joel Marks and Roger Ames, 65–90. New York: State University of New York Press.

Blair, James, Derek Mitchell, and Karina Blair. 2005. *The Psychopath: Emotion and the Brain*. Malden, MA: Blackwell.

Block, N. 2010. "Attention and Mental Paint." *Philosophical Issues* 20 (1): 23–63.

Blum, Lawrence. 1994. *Moral Perception and Particularity*. New York: Cambridge University Press.

Bommarito, Nicolas. 2017. "Virtuous and Vicious Anger." *Journal of Ethics and Social Philosophy* 11 (3).

———. 2016. "Private Solidarity." *Ethical Theory and Moral Practice* 19 (2):445–455.

———. 2013. "Modesty as a Virtue of Attention." *Philosophical Review* 122 (1): 93–117.

———. 2011. "Bile & Bodhisattvas: Śantideva on Justified Anger." *Journal of Buddhist Ethics* 18:357–381.

Buddhaghosa. 1999. *The Path of Purification (Visugghimagga)*. Translated by Bikkhu Nanamoli. Onalaska: Buddhist Publication Society.

Capps, Lisa, Nurit Yirmiya, and Marian Sigman. 1992. "Understanding of Simple and Complex Emotions in Non-retarded Children with Autism." *Journal of Child Psychology and Psychiatry* 33 (7): 1169–1182.

Carnegie, Dale. 1936/1981. *How to Win Friends and Influence People*. New York: Pocket Books.

Charland, Louis C. 1997. "Reconciling Cognitive and Perceptual Theories of Emotion: A Representational Proposal." *Philosophy of Science* 64 (4): 555–579.

Chisholm, Nick, and Grant Gillett. 2005. "The Patient's Journey: Living with Locked-In Syndrome." *British Medical Journal* 331 (7508): 94–97.

Comte-Sponville, André. 1996/2001. *A Small Treatise on the Great Virtues*. Translated by Catherine Temerson. New York: Metropolitan/Owl Books.

Conze, Edward. 1967/1973. *Buddhist Thought in India*. Ann Arbor: University of Michigan Press.

D'Arms, Justin, and Daniel Jacobson. 2000. "The Moralistic Fallacy: On the 'Appropriateness' of Emotions." *Philosophy and Phenomenological Research* 61 (1): 65–90.

Darwall, Stephen. 2006. *The Second-Person Standpoint*. Cambridge, MA: Harvard University Press.

———. 2002. *Welfare and Rational Care*. Princeton, NJ: Princeton University Press.

———. 1997/1998. "Empathy, Sympathy, and Care." *Philosophical Studies* 89 (2/3): 261–282.

DeBrabander, Firmin. 2004. "Psychotherapy and Moral Perfection." In *Stoicism*, edited by Steven Strange and Jack Zupko, 198–213. Cambridge: Cambridge University Press.

Dennett, Daniel. 2007. "Thank Goodness!" In *Philosophers without gods: Meditations on Atheism and the Secular Life*, edited by Louise Antony, 113–120. New York: Oxford University Press.

Descartes, René. 1649/1985. *Passions of the Soul*. In *The Philosophical Writings of Descartes*, Volume I, 325–404. Translated by John Cottingham, Robert Stoothoff, and Dugald Murdoch. Cambridge: Cambridge University Press.

De Sousa, Ronald. 1990. *The Rationality of Emotion*. Cambridge, MA: The MIT Press.

Doris, John. 2005. *Lack of Character*. Cambridge: Cambridge University Press.

Driver, Julia. 2016. "Minimal Virtue." *The Monist* 99 (2): 97–111.

———. 2007. "Dream Immorality." *Philosophy* 34 (3): 5–22.

———. 2001. *Uneasy Virtue*. New York: Cambridge University Press.

———. 1996. "The Virtues and Human Nature." In *How Should One Live?*, edited by Roger Crisp, 111–130. Oxford: Clarendon Press.

———. 1989. "The Virtues of Ignorance." *The Journal of Philosophy* 86 (7): 373–384.

Durso, Geoffrey R. O., Andrew Luttrell, and Baldwin M. Way. 2015. "Over-the-Counter Relief from Pains and Pleasures Alike: Acetaminophen Blunts Evaluation Sensitivity to Both Negative and Positive Stimuli." *Psychological Science* 26 (6): 750–758.

Ekman, Paul. 1992a. "Are There Basic Emotions?" *Psychological Review* 99 (3): 550–553.

———. 1992b. "An Argument for Basic Emotions." *Cognition and Emotion* 6 (3/4): 169–200.

Elman, Michael J., Joel Sugar, Richard Fiscella, Thomas A. Deutsch, James Noth, Michael Nyberg, Kirk Packo, and Robert J. Anderson. 1998. "The Effect of Propranolol Versus Placebo on Resident Surgical Performance." *Transactions of the American Ophthalmological Society* 96:283–294.

Epictetus. 2008. *Discourses and Selected Writings*. Translated by Robert Dobbin. New York: Penguin Classics.

Elster, Jon. 2004. "Emotion and Action." In *Thinking About Feeling*, edited by Robert Solomon, 151–162. New York: Oxford University Press.

Everitt, Nicholas. 2007. "Some Problems with Virtue Theory." *Philosophy* 82:275–299.

Farrell, Daniel. 1980. "Jealousy." *The Philosophical Review* 89 (4): 527–559.

Fitzgerald, Patrick. 1998. "Gratitude and Justice." *Ethics* 109 (1): 119–153.

Flanagan, Owen. 1991. *Varieties of Moral Personality*. Cambridge, MA: Harvard University Press.

———. 1990. "Virtue and Ignorance." *The Journal of Philosophy* 87:420–428.

Foot, Philippa. 2001. *Natural Goodness*. New York: Oxford University Press.

———. 1979. "Virtues and Vices." In *Virtues and Vices and Other Essays in Moral Philosophy*, 8–14. Berkeley: University of California Press.

Frankfurt, Harry. 2006. *The Reasons of Love*. Princeton, NJ: Princeton University Press.

———. 1999. "On Caring." In *Necessity, Volition, and Love*, 155–180. New York: Cambridge University Press.

———. 1982/1988. "The Importance of What We Care About." In *The Importance of What We Care About*, 80–94. New York: Cambridge University Press.

Frijda, Nico. 2007. *The Laws of Emotion*. Mahwah, NJ: Lawrence Erlbaum.

———. 1987. *The Emotions*. Cambridge: Cambridge University Press.

Frost, Randy, and Gail Steketee. 2010. *Stuff: Compulsive Hoarding and the Meaning of Things*. New York: Houghton Mifflin Harcourt.

Ganeri, Jonardon. 2017. *Attention Not Self*. New York: Oxford University Press.

Garfield, Jay. 2015. *Engaging Buddhism*. New York: Oxford University Press.

Gendler, Tamar Szabó. 2011. "On the Epistemic Costs of Implicit Bias." *Philosophical Studies* 156 (1): 33–63.

Gibbard, Allan. 2003. *Thinking How to Live*. Cambridge, MA: Harvard University Press.

Gilovich, Thomas. 1991. *How We Know What Isn't So*. New York: Free Press.

Gyalsé Thogmé (rGyal sras thog med). 2005. *rGyal ba'i sras kyi lag len sum cu so bdun ma*. Chengdu: People's Press.

Hacker-Wright, John. 2010. "Virtue Ethics Without Right Action: Anscombe, Foot, and Contemporary Virtue Ethics." *The Journal of Value Inquiry* 44:209–224.

Hare, Robert D. 1993. *Without Conscience*. New York: The Guilford Press.

Harman, Gilbert. 1999. "Moral Philosophy Meets Social Psychology: Virtue Ethics and the Fundamental Attribution Error." *Proceedings of the Aristotelian Society* 99:315–331.

Heider, F. 1958. *The Psychology of Interpersonal Relations*. New York: Wiley.

Heim, Maria. 2012. "Shame and Apprehension: Notes on the Moral Value of Hiri and Ottappa." In *Embedded Languages: Studies in the Religion, Culture, and History of Sri Lanka*, edited by Carol S. Anderson, Susanne Mrozik, W. M. Wijeratna, and R. M. W. Rajapaksha, 237–260. Colombo, Sri Lanka: Godage Books.

Held, Virginia. 2006. *The Ethics of Care*. New York: Oxford University Press.

Herpertz, Sabine, and Henning Sass. 2000. "Emotional Deficiency and Psychopathy." *Behavioral Sciences and the Law* 18:576–580.

Hibbs, Darren. 2010. "A Conceptual Analysis of Clutch Performances in Competitive Sports." *Journal of the Philosophy of Sport* 37 (1): 47–59.

Hill, Thomas E. 1991. "Servility and Self-Respect." In *Autonomy and Self-Respect*, 4–18. Cambridge: Cambridge University Press.

Hume, David. 1978. *A Treatise of Human Nature*. New York: Oxford University Press.

Hurka, Thomas. 2010. "Right Act, Virtuous Motive." *Metaphilosophy* 41:58–72.

———. 2001. *Virtue, Vice, and Value*. New York: Oxford University Press.

Hursthouse, Rosalind. 1999. *On Virtue Ethics*. Oxford: Oxford University Press.

———. 1996. "Normative Virtue Ethics." In *How Should One Live?*, edited by Roger Crisp. 19–36. Oxford: Clarendon Press.

Jackson, Natasha. 1971. "Unselfish Joy: A Neglected Virtue." In *Mudita: The Buddha's Teaching on Unselfish Joy*. Kandy, Sri Lanka: Buddhist Publication Society. http://www.accesstoinsight.org/lib/authors/various/wheel170. html#neglected.

James, William. 1892/1992. *Psychology: The Briefer Course*. In *William James: Writings 1878–1899*. New York: The Library of America.

———. 1890/2007. *The Principles of Psychology, Volume 1*. New York: Cosimo.

———. 1884. "What Is an Emotion?" *Mind* 9:188–205.

Keeler, J. J. 2012. *I Hardly Ever Wash My Hands*. St. Paul, MN: Paragon House.

Kelly, Thomas. 2008. "Disagreement, Dogmatism, and Belief Polarization." *Journal of Philosophy* 105 (10): 611–633.

Kenny, Anthony. 1963. *Action, Emotion and Will*. London: Routledge & Keegan Paul.

Kluger, Jeffrey. 2001. "The Post-Bin Laden Party—And Why You Should Enjoy It." *Time Magazine*, May 4.

Koch, Christof. 2004. *The Quest for Consciousness*. Englewood, NJ: Roberts and Company.

Korsgaard, Christine, M. 1996. *The Sources of Normativity*. Cambridge: Cambridge University Press.

Kosman, L.A. 1980. "On Being Properly Affected: Virtues and Feelings in Aristotle's Ethics." In *Essays on Aristotle's Ethics*, edited by Amélie Rorty. 103–116. Berkeley: University of California Press.

Kotchoubey, Boris, and Martin Lotze. 2013. "Instrumental Methods in the Diagnostics of Locked-In Syndrome." *Restorative Neurology and Neuroscience* 31 (1): 25–40.

Lange, Carl. 1885/1922. *Om Sindsbevaegelser: et Psyko-Fysiologisk Studie*. Kjbenhavn: Jacob Lunds. Reprinted in 1922. *The Emotions*. Edited by Carl Lange and William James. Translated by I. A. Haupt. 33–92. Baltimore: Williams & Wilkins Company.

Langri Tangpa (Glang ri thang pa). 2010. *Blo sbyong tshigs rkang brgyad ma* in *Blo spyong brgya rtsa phyogs sgrig*. Lhasa: Tibet People's Press.

Laureys, Steven, Frédéric Pellas, Philippe Van Eeckhout, Sofiane Ghorbel, Caroline Schnakers, Fabien Perrin, Jacques Berre, et al. (2005) "The Locked-In Syndrome: What Is It Like to Be Conscious but Paralyzed and Voiceless?" *Progress in Brain Research* 150:495–611.

Liezi. 1960. *The Book of Lieh-tsu*. Translated by A. C. Graham. New York: Columbia University Press.

Long, A. A. 2002. *Epictetus*. Oxford: Clarendon Press.

————. 1996. *Stoic Studies*. Cambridge: Cambridge University Press.

Losh, Molly, and Lisa Capps. 2006. "Understanding of Emotional Experience in Autism: Insights from the Personal Accounts of High-Functioning Children with Autism." *Developmental Psychology* 42 (5): 809–818.

Lycan, William. 1988. *Judgment and Justification*. New York: Cambridge University Press.

Mack, Arien, and Irvin Rock. 1998. *Inattentional Blindness*. Cambridge, MA: MIT Press.

Maguire, Barry. 2016. "Love in the Time of Consequentialism." *Noûs*. doi: 10.1111/nous.12169

Marks, Joel. 1982. "A Theory of Emotion." *Philosophical Studies* 42 (2): 227–242.

Mayberry, Stephanie. 2012. "Alien: A Story of Asperger's Syndrome." In *First Person Accounts of Mental Illness and Recovery*, edited by Craig Winston LeCroy and Jane Holschuh, 431–440. Hoboken, NJ: John Wiley and Sons.

McCarty, Richard R. 1993. "Kantian Moral Motivation and the Feeling of Respect." *Journal of the History of Philosophy* 31 (3): 421–435.

McConnell, Terrance. 1993. *Gratitude*. Philadelphia: Temple University Press.

McIntosh, Peggy. 1988. "White Privilege: Unpacking the Invisible Knapsack." In 2007. *Race, Class, and Gender in the United States: An Integrated Study*, Vol. 1, No. 3, Macmillan 177–182.

Mele, Alfred. 2001. *Self-Deception Unmasked*. Princeton, NJ: Princeton University Press.

Mengzi. 2009. *Mencius*. Translated by Irene Bloom. New York: Columbia University Press.

Miles, Siân. 1986. "Introduction." In *Simone Weil: An Anthology*, edited by Siân Miles, 1–68. London: Virago.

Mole, Christopher. 2007. "Attention, Self, and the Sovereignty of Good." In *Iris Murdoch: A Reassessment*, edited by Anne Rowe, 72–84. New York: Palgrave Macmillan.

Moore, G. E. 1903/1993. *Principia Ethica*. Cambridge: Cambridge University Press.

Moray, N. 1959. "Attention and Dichotic Listening: Affective Cues and the Influence of Instructions." *Quarterly Journal of Experimental Psychology* 11:56–60.

Murdoch, Iris. 1964/2001. "The Idea of Perfection" in *The Sovereignty of the Good*. 1–44. New York: Routledge.

Nickerson, R. S. 1998. "Confirmation Bias: A Ubiquitous Phenomenon in Many Guises." *Review of General Psychology* 2 (2): 175–220.

Noddings, Nel. 1984/2003. *Caring*. Berkeley: University of California Press.

Nozick, Robert. 1974. *Anarchy, State, and Utopia*. New York: Basic Books.

Nuyen, A. T. 1998. "Just Modesty." *American Philosophical Quarterly* 35 (1): 101–109.

Oates, L. R. 1971. "The Nature and Implications of Mudita." In *Mudita: The Buddha's Teaching on Unselfish Joy*. Kandy: Buddhist Publication Society.

Oatley, Keith, Dacher Keltner, and Jennifer Jenkins. 2006. *Understanding Emotions*. Malden, MA: Blackwell.

Patterson, J. R., and M. Grabois. 1986. "Locked-In Syndrome: A Review of 139 Cases." *Stroke* 17:758–764.

Perkins, Judith. 1995. *The Suffering Self*. New York: Routledge.

Pétrement, Simone. 1976/1988. *Simone Weil: A Life*. New York: Schocken Books.

Pistorius, Martin. 2013. *Ghost Boy*. Nashville, TN: Nelson Books.

Portmann, John. 2000. *When Bad Things Happen to Other People*. New York: Routledge.

Posner, Michael. 1980. "Orienting of Attention." *Quarterly Journal of Experimental Psychology* 32:3–25.

Prinz, Jesse. 2011. *The Conscious Brain*. New York: Oxford University Press.

———. 2004a. "Embodied Emotions." In *Thinking About Feeling*, edited by Robert Solomon, 44–60. New York: Oxford University Press.

———. 2004b. *Gut Reactions: A Perceptual Theory of Emotion*. New York: Oxford University Press.

Rashdall, Hastings. 1907. *The Theory of Good and Evil*. Oxford: Clarendon Press.

Raterman, Ty. 2006. "On Modesty: Being Good and Knowing It Without Flaunting It." *American Philosophical Quarterly* 43:221–234.

Rawls, John. 1971/1999. *A Theory of Justice*. Cambridge, MA: Belknap Press.

Ridge, Michael. 2000. "Modesty as a Virtue." *American Philosophical Quarterly* 37 (3): 269–283.

Roberts, Robert. 2003. *Emotions: An Essay in Moral Psychology*. Cambridge: Cambridge University Press.

———. 1988. "What an Emotion Is: A Sketch." *The Philosophical Review* 97 (2): 183–209.

Ronson, Jon. 2011. *The Psychopath Test*. New York: Riverhead Books.

Ross, W. D. 1936/1963. *Foundations of Ethics*. Oxford: Clarendon Press.

Russell, Daniel C. 2009. *Practical Intelligence and the Virtues*. Oxford: Oxford University Press.

Sacks, Oliver. 1995. *An Anthropologist on Mars*. New York: Vintage.

Śāntideva (*Zhi ba lha*). 2004. *Byang chub sems dpa'i spyod pa la 'jug pa* (*Bodhicaryāvatāra*). Varanasi: Vajra Vidya Institute Library.

Sartre, Jean-Paul. 1948/1993. *The Emotions: Outline of a Theory*. Translated by Bernard Frechtman. Secaucus, NJ: Citadel Press.

Sayadaw, U Pandita. 2006. *A State of Mind Called Beautiful*. Boston: Wisdom Publications.

Scanlon, Thomas. 2008. *Moral Dimensions*. Cambridge, MA: The Belknap Press of Harvard University Press.

Schopenhauer, Arthur. 1839/1995. *On the Basis of Morality*. Translated by E. F. J. Payne. Indianapolis: Hackett.

Schramme, Thomas. (ed.) 2014. *Being Amoral: Psychopathy and Moral Incapacity*. Cambridge, MA: The MIT Press.

Schroeder, Timothy. 2004. *Three Faces of Desire*. New York: Oxford University Press.

Shamay-Tsoory, Simone. 2008. "Recognition of 'Fortune of Others' Emotions in Asperger Syndrome and High Functioning Autism." *The Journal of Autism and Developmental Disorders* 38:1451–1461.

Sher, George. 2006. In *Praise of Blame*. New York: Oxford University Press.

———. 2002. "Blameworthy Action and Character." *Philosophy and Phenomenological Research* 64 (2): 381–392.

Sidgwick, Henry. 1907/1982. *The Methods of Ethics*. Indianapolis: Hackett.

Simmons, A. John. 1979. *Moral Principles and Political Obligations*. Princeton: Princeton University Press.

Slote, Michael. 2007. *The Ethics of Care and Empathy*. London: Routledge.

———. 1983. *Goods and Virtue*. Oxford: Clarendon Press.

Solomon, Robert. 2007. *True to Our Feelings*. New York: Oxford University Press.

———. 1998. "The Virtues of a Passionate Life: Erotic Love and 'The Will to Power'" *Social Philosophy and Policy* 15:91–118.

Sorensen, Roy. 1988. *Blindspots*. Oxford: Clarendon Press.

Spinoza, Benedict De. 1677/1996. *Ethics*. Translated by Edwin Curley. New York: Penguin Classics.

Sprengelmeyer, R., Young, A., Schroeder, U., Grossenbacher, P., Federlein, J., Büttner, T., and Przuntek, H. 1999. "Knowing No Fear." *Proceedings of the Royal Society of London B: Biological Sciences* 266:2451–2456.

Stangl, Rebecca. 2010 "Asymmetrical Virtue Particularism." *Ethics* 121:37–57.

Stazicker, J. 2011. "Attention, Visual Consciousness and Indeterminacy." *Mind & Language* 26 (2): 156–184.

Strawson, Galen. 1994. *Mental Reality*. Cambridge, MA: MIT Press.

Strawson, Peter. 1962. "Freedom and Resentment." In 2003. *Free Will edited by* Gary Watson, 72–94. New York: Oxford University Press.

Svensson, Frans. 2010. "Virtue Ethics and the Search for an Account of Right Action." *Ethical Theory and Moral Practice* 13:255–271.

Summers, Jesse and Walter Sinnott-Armstrong. Forthcoming. *Too Much Morality: Philosophical Reflections on Scrupulosity.*

Swanton, Christine. 2003. *Virtue Ethics: A Pluralistic View*. New York: Oxford University Press.

Tavalaro, Julia, and Richard Tayson. 1997. *Look Up for Yes*. New York: Penguin Books.

Taylor, Blake. 2007. *ADHD and Me*. Oakland, CA: New Harbinger.

Taylor, Gabriele. 2006. *Deadly Vices*. Oxford: Clarendon Press.

Tessman, Lisa. 2005. *Burdened Virtues: Virtue Ethics for Liberatory Struggles*. New York: Oxford University Press.

Thagard, Paul. 2006. "Desires Are Not Propositional Attitudes." *Dialogue* 45:151–156.

Thompson, J. J. T. 1997. "The Right and the Good." *The Journal of Philosophy* 94 (6): 273–298.

Traig, Jennifer. 2004. *Devil in the Details*. New York: Back Bay Books.

Tsai, Jeanne L., Robert W. Levenson, and Kimberly McCoy. 2006. "Cultural and Temperamental Variation in Emotional Response." *Emotion* 6 (3): 484–497.

Tversky, Amos, and Daniel Kahneman. 1974. "Judgment Under Uncertainty: Heuristics and Biases." *Science* 185 (4157): 1124–1131.

Valentine, Vikki, and Jon Hamilton. 2006. "Q&A: Temple Grandin on Autism & Language." National Public Radio. Available at http://www.npr.org/templates/story/story.php?storyId=5488844. Accessed on December 1, 2012.

van Zyl, Liezl. 2011. "Right Action and the Non-Virtuous Agent." *Journal of Applied Philosophy* 28:80–92.

———. 2009. "Agent-Based Virtue Ethics and the Problem of Action Guidance." *Journal of Moral Philosophy* 6:50–69.

Velleman, David. 2013. "Sociality and Solitude." *Philosophical Explorations* 16 (3): 324–335.

Walker, A. D. M. 1980. "Gratefulness and Gratitude." *Proceedings of the Aristotelian Society* 81:39–55.

Walton, Kendall. 1990. *Mimesis as Make-Believe*. Cambridge, MA: Harvard University Press.

Watzl, S. 2011. "Attention as Structuring of the Stream of Consciousness." In *Attention: Philosophical and Psychological Essays*, edited by Christopher Mole, Declan Smithies, and Wayne Wu, 145–173. New York: Oxford University Press.

Weeks, Linton. 2011, May 2. "Is It Wrong to Celebrate Osama Bin Laden's Death?" National Public Radio. Available at http://www.npr.org/2011/05/03/135927693/is-it-wrong-to-celebrate-bin-ladens-death

Weil, Simone. 1947/1999. *Gravity and Grace*. Translated by Emma Crawford and Mario von der Ruhr. New York: Routledge.

Wender, Paul. 2001. *Attention-Deficit Hyperactivity Disorder in Children, Adolescents, and Adults*. New York: Oxford University Press.

Whiteman, Thomas, and Michele Novonti. 1995. *Adult ADD*. Colorado Springs, CO: Pinon Press.

Williams, Bernard. 1985/1998. *Ethics and the Limits of Philosophy*. Cambridge, MA: Harvard University Press.

———. 1981. "Utilitarianism and Moral Self-Indulgence." In *Moral Luck*, 45–47. Cambridge: Cambridge University Press.

———. 1973/1988. "Consequentialism and Integrity." In *Consequentialism and Its Critics*, edited by Samuel Scheffler, 20–50. New York: Oxford University Press.

Winston, Wayne. 2012. *Mathletics*. Princeton, NJ: Princeton University Press.

Wolf, Susan. 2011. "Blame, Italian Style." In *Reason and Recognition: Essays on the Philosophy of T. M. Scanlon*, edited by R. J. Wallace, R. Kumar, and S. Freeman, 332–347. New York: Oxford University Press.

———. 1982. "Moral Saints." *The Journal of Philosophy* 79 (8): 419–439.

Wu, Wayne. 2014. *Attention*. New York: Routledge.

———. 2011a. "What Is Conscious Attention?" *Philosophy and Phenomenological Research* 82 (1): 93–120.

———. 2011b. "Attention as Selection for Action." In *Attention: Philosophical and Psychological Essays*, edited by Christopher Mole, Declan Smithies, and Wayne Wu, 97–116. New York: Oxford University Press.

Young, Susan, and Jessica Bramham. 2007. *ADHD in Adults: A Psychological Guide to Practice*. Chichester, England: John Wiley & Sons.

Zimmerman, Dean W. 1997. "Immanent Causation." *Philosophical Perspectives* 11:433–471.

INDEX

abandoned spoon, 119, 122
acedia, 88n13
action
    attention and, 130–131, 142–144, 165
    covert and overt, 8, 14–15, 130
    emotions and, 87–89
    moral assessment of, 1–2
    moral theory and, 11–13, 171
    virtue and, 7, 12, 15, 20, 33, 38, 171
    voluntary and involuntary, 8–9, 173–174
Adams, Robert, 6n7, 13n3, 23n14, 35n24,
    48n4, 85n5, 90n16, 135n13
ADD. *See* attention-deficit disorder
aidōs, 90n17
Allport, D. A., 130n6
anger, 8–9, 31–32, 35, 41, 84–85, 91,
    93, 97–99, 101–102, 106, 113n56,
    123, 125
Annas, Julia, 7n8, 13n3, 23n14
annoyance, 9, 45, 76, 91, 104
anorexia, 93–94
Anscombe, Elizabeth, 12–13
Aquinas, Thomas, 64–65, 117, 70n25, 89n15
Aristotle, 5, 13n2, 39–40, 44n1, 57n14, 77,
    89n14, 89n15, 109–110, 113
Arpaly, Nomy, 6n7, 24, 57, 58n15, 86n9
attention
    action and, 130–131, 142–144, 165
    auditory, 130, 138

awareness and, 128
beliefs and, 140–141
care and, 137–141, 169–170
charity and, 115
duration of, 131
features of, 128–132
frequency of, 146–147
gaze and, 129
gratitude and, 148–160
lack of, 164–165
love and, 137–138
modesty and, 160–169
overt and covert, 130–131
patterns of, 131, 164–165
unexpressed in action, 143
voluntary and involuntary,
    130–131, 131n7
attention-deficit disorder, 39–40, 135–136,
    163–164
    firsthand accounts of, 136n15
Aurelius, Marcus, 157n37
Austen, Jane, 115
autism, 39, 108–113, 123–124
    moral character and, 110–113

Baez, Joan, 61
Baier, Annette, 5n6, 84n4, 85n6, 91
Baker, Judith, 116n61
Baron, James, 140n21